SOCIAL PROBLEMS

SOCIAL PROBLEMS

Satish Mittal
Sushil Kumar Saxena

Commonwealth

Social Problems

First Published : 2012

ISBN 978-81-311-0372-2

Published by :
COMMONWEALTH PUBLISHERS PVT. LTD.
4831/24, Prahlad Street,
Ansari Road, Darya Ganj,
New Delhi - 110002
Ph. : 23272541, 23257835
Fax : 91- 011- 23257835
e-mail : commonwealthbooks@gmail.com

Laser Typesetting by :
Dimple Computers
Delhi

Printed at :
Roshan Offset Printers
Delhi

Preface

Social issues are matters which directly or indirectly affect a person or many members of a society and are considered to be problems, controversies related to moral values, or both. Our society consists of people from different religious, linguistic and ethnic backgrounds and we are currently experiencing social tensions of various kinds. They are related to the pattern of social change. In particular the rise of middle class migration of people from villages to cities, increase in the degree of economic inequality, spread of education and media are playing key role. The tensions in the lives of people at individual, family and community level is clearly visible. Most of the conflicts and tensions revolve around the issue of identity.

In this modern world, it is inevitable that many of the social problems which have so far been seen as national in character will assume a global character. Global social problems are those which cannot be confined within national boundaries and which need both national and international attention if they are to be ameliorated.

This book provides an original and much-needed introduction to global social problems. The most important global social issues are explored and suggestions to recover from each problems are also described. It will be essential reading for undergraduate students in the social science, particularly those studying social policy, sociology and politics.

Contents

1

Introduction to Social Problems

India is one of the developing nations of the modern world. It has become an independent country, a republic, more than a half century ago. During this period the country has been engaged in efforts to attain development and growth in various areas such as building infrastructure, production of food grains, science and technology and spread of education. The life expectancy has increased and many diseases have been controlled. However, there are many areas in which Indian society is experiencing a variety of problems. Some of these problems have their roots in our colonial past while others are related to demographic changes, sociopolitical conditions and cultural processes.

Poverty

A large section of the Indian society is suffering from poverty. Poverty is a phenomenon which is objective as well a subjective. Objectively poverty implies a dehumanising condition in which people are unable to look after the basic needs. Subjectively poverty stands for perceived deprivation. As such it is relative and any body can feel poor by comparing himself as herself with a rich person. Poor people lack the necessary resources and capacity to satisfy basic needs like food, shelter, health and education. They live under difficult conditions which are not conducive for development of their human potential. Poverty interferes with development in many ways. For instance lack of or inadequate nutrition arrests mental development during early childhood. The unavailability of stimulating environment and absence of effective role models decreases the motivation level.

A large section of poor children do not go to school. Even if they go they become drop out and fail to complete education. In this context it may be pointed out that poverty is also related to the social structure. A number of low caste, scheduled tribe and backward communities have been put to discrimination for many centuries. They are socially disadvantaged and are deprived from the experiences necessary for development on account of their membership of specific groups. In this sense they are doubly deprived.

Studies have shown that the children from the background of poverty and social disadvantage flag behind their counterparts from the enriched background. Their cognitive development and performance is found to be at a lower level. Studies of perception, memory an intelligence have demonstrated it several times. The studies have also shown that the performance between the advantaged and disadvantaged children increases with advancing age. It has also been found that the poverty condition is de-motivating and makes a person more vulnerable. Low level of achievement motivation and greater need for dependence in these people make them less effective in coping with the problems of every day life. As a result the poor become marginalised and can not contribute to the mainstream of the society.

The question why some people are poor has been answered in many ways. The search for causes of poverty has lead to many answers. It has been located in the individual, in the social structure, or the culture of the people. For instance many people blame the victim and consider the poor as responsible for the characteristics or dispositions of the people. A detailed analysis of the problem of poverty shows that poverty is caused by multiple factors. The social and economic structure in India promotes inequality, and social disadvantages. The life in the poverty condition reinforces certain behaviour pattern, values and coping styles which, reduce the chances of upward social mobility.

SOCIAL TENSIONS

The Indian society consists of people from different religious, linguistic and ethnic backgrounds. Since long there has been cultural give and take between the people from India and other countries. Since 1947 when India gained political independence the country has been engaged in the gigantic task of nation building. Efforts have been made to put nation on the path of socioeconomic development.

The transformation of nation as a self sufficient and cohesive political entity has proved to be a difficult challenge. The colonial past, socioeconomic disparities in the society and raised aspirations have culminated in a complex situation. Traditionally the Indian society was hierarchically arranged and the different communities and caste groups showed a pattern of social distance in which low caste, tribes and minority groups were discriminated against and looked down upon. Many of the communities were considered as untouchable.

The Indian constitution prohibits against such discrimination and has abolished untouchability. However, it is still practised in certain ways. All these condition have created a situation in which various kinds of social tensions have become very frequent events are as follows:

— If we look at the historical trends we notice that the partition of India led to considerable degree of violence and the harmonious relations between Hindus and Muslims were disturbed. As a result suspicion and mistrust has developed between Muslims and Hindus. This has led to a number of clashes and conflicts which have been violent and have generated hatred.

— Various parts of the country are experiencing separatist movements. You must have read about political movements in North East part of India (Assam, Nagaland, Tripura) where demands for separate political identities have been raised from time to time. The Kashmir region is experiencing the negative impact of cross-border terrorism and people are suffering. The Nuxalite movement in certain parts (Andhra Pradesh, Bihar, Madhya Pradesh) is also creating political instability and problems of governance.

— Caste-related prejudice and discrimination has also been on rise in certain parts of the country. In the course of socialisation people acquire negative attitudes and stereotypes. Many times these are not founded in our real life experiences. Instead, they are based on false information, personal impressions and hearsay. However, they are very powerful and shape our behaviour in important ways. Thus if we have prejudice against some one it may lead to aggression, hostility and harm doing towards the target groups. In recent years inter group conflicts related to caste have moved from the social to the political arena of life. In fact caste based alliances, groups and organisation are growing fast. They utilise caste-related identity for political gains. Today caste-affiliations are not so important in social or religious matters as they are in political matters. In this context the rise of low caste groups who often call them selves Dalits is becoming a prominent feature of modern India. The presence of this group has changed the complexion of Indian political scene.

On the whole the Indian society is currently experiencing social tensions of various kinds. They are related to the pattern of social change. In particular the rise of middle class migration of people from villages to cities, increase in the degree of economic inequality, spread of education and media are playing key role. The tensions in the lives of people at individual, family and community level is clearly visible.

Most of the conflicts and tensions revolve around the issue of identity. Assertion of separate identity and promoting the same with different tactics is becoming a central problem. People use identities in an emotionally charged way to create a group structure for promoting certain goals. Thus associations, committees and organisations are created to serve these purposes. The creation of identity involves strategies which enhance similarity within the group and difference between the groups. In this way a diversion of "in group" or "own group and "out group" or other group is created. This kind of differentiation is present in almost all societies. This also implies that the differences across groups cannot be totally eliminated.

Some psychological intervention for enhancing group behaviour Since groups are inevitable and constitute an important part of our social reality what we need is to recognise the essence and value of pluralism. All groups are important and play distinct role. We need to appreciate this diversity in our social life in a positive manner. The approach should be to evolve a strategy in which diverse groups and communities are able to live distinct patterns of life the way they want. The various groups or communities should compliment each other and help in achieving their goals. Super ordinate goals may be created that may be shared by all the groups. To this end the following steps may prove very helpful.

- Increasing dialogue amongst the diverse groups existing in the society.
- Building an atmosphere of mutual trust and harmony.
- Equity and equality of opportunity for different groups needs to be ensured.
- Greater opportunities for mutual care, respect and complementary need to be created.

Gender Discrimination

Women and men are equally important for the growth and development of individual and social lives. The women play the important role as mother and the same makes it unique. However, careful analysis of Indian society indicates that the situation is not good for women folk. The sex ratio of male and female in the India population has been changing and becoming unfavourable towards women. In the Indian society women are considered major contributors to family and society.

We have gods and goddesses both and one of the incarnation of lord Shiva is Ardhanareeshwar, which is made of half male and half female in its constitution. Unfortunately this equality and prominence tells an incomplete fact. The women are also subjected to discrimination in learning, dowry deaths and expatiations of various kinds which are very common. In fact the women are becoming targets of atrocities of many types. The same is manifested in discrimination against them from very early period. The incident of infanticide, early marriage, emphasis on domestic activities and lessor emphasis on education and career have made women's lives full of problems.

They are discriminated against from early childhood. The Indian dependence on others (e.g. parents, husbands) becomes fate of the majority of the women folk. The pattern of discrimination against women varies across rural, urban and tribal areas. They are assigned diverse responsibilities and treated as relatively weaker and less competent. This image is still prevailing in various sections of the society. It is reflected in the discriminatory practices in the family such as distribution of work, food and social activities. The girl child is usually burdened with responsibilities that are beyond her capacity. Such exploitation function as obstacles in the process of development and growth of the girl child.

When a girl child matures and becomes an adult she is often found to be physically weak and mentally constrained. They are neither able to realise their potential nor able to contribute to the mainstream of society. Their contributions are often limited to family and that too are ignored.

However, some Indian women have been able to overcome the barriers in their path and became successful in many walks of life. In this connection one can mention the names of Pandita Rama Bai, Sarojini Naidu, Indira Gandhi who emerged as leaders at national level. The provision for education, legal provisions about the age of marriage and reservation for women in various walks of life has contributed to change in their situation. Today the presence of women in various occupations and public offices is much more prominent than what it used to be during earlier periods. However, the Indian society has still to go a long way as for as gender equality is concerned.

Corruption, Illiteracy and Urbanisation

As a developing country India is facing a number of problems which need careful analysis and demands steps for their solution. These problems are many in number. The salient ones include corruption, illiteracy and urbanisation. Let us briefly discuss these problems. Corruption refers to those transactions which involve unduc benefits to some people who don't deserve or are not entitled for them.

Such transactions make some people recipients of financial benefits, physical and social resources that make these people capable of exhorting power over others and controlling the rewards and punishments for others. This is often reflected in the formation of a nexus between politicians and criminals. Use of money to bribe and drawing benefits that are not feasible under the law of the land. Misuse and misappropriation of resources for personal benefits is creating a gulf between "haves" and "have not". The use of black money and scans of various types that have been discovered in recent years clearly tell that corruption is adversely influencing the growth and development of Indian society.

Illiteracy is another major problem before the society. It's a sad state of affairs that a country which had higher level of literacy (than British) at a time when British came two centuries ago is now facing the challenge of a huge number of people who are illiterate and cannot read or write. The lack of these skills renders them deprived of the opportunities for upward social mobility. Such people have to depend on others for various things and are exploited in various ways. For example the poor rural people are asked to put their thumb impression of various legal documents and are subjected to exploitation and legal hassles.

Keeping these negative consequences in view the government is trying to universes primary education. The lack of reading and writing skills makes a person incapable of availing the various opportunities to help themselves. Each and every educated person, therefore, is expected to contribute to the literacy mission and making it a success. Urbanisation is another problem that deserves serious attention. There is increasingly greater migration from villages to cities. This situation is generating pressures on cities which were meant for a definite size of population.

The limited civic facilities, civilian organisations and structures are facing difficulties in meeting the demands of the people. The mega cities like Mumbai, Kolkata Chennai and Delhi have crossed the limits for which they are capable of. This situation creates a number of problems such as unauthorised and illegal activities, emergence of slums, problem of waste disposal creation of floes, crime and health related problems. The social organisation, economy and environmental planning in many cities are becoming unmanageable.

Also, urbanisation is linked with certain kinds of attitude like consumerism and individualism. Consumerism emphasises on exploitation of resources for personal consumption without any concern for society and environment. This attitude is responsible for the ecological imbalance that is widely experienced in today's world. Similarly the individualistic attitude favours the view that the individual is the ultimate reality and all processes need to be explained at individual level. The individual is free and responsible to his or her self only.

The social problems described above deal with different domains of life. You can see that the solutions for these problems require inputs from different disciplines. The role of psychology is prominent as it deals with behaviour. Modification of attitudes, feelings and pattern of behaviour are significant. Psychologists can contribute by providing strategies for achieving these goals.

2

Issue of Poverty

Poverty is the lack of basic human needs, such as clean water, nutrition, health care, education, clothing and shelter, because of the inability to afford them. This is also referred to as absolute poverty or destitution. Relative poverty is the condition of having fewer resources or less income than others within a society or country, or compared to worldwide averages. About 1.7 billion people live in absolute poverty; before the industrial revolution, poverty had mostly been the norm.

Poverty reduction has historically been a result of economic growth as increased levels of production, such as modern industrial technology, made more wealth available for those who were otherwise too poor to afford them. Also, investments in modernising agriculture and increasing yields is considered the core of the anti-poverty effort, given three-quarters of the world's poor are rural farmers.

Today, continued economic development is constrained by the lack of economic freedom. Economic liberalisation includes extending property rights, especially to land, to the poor, and making financial services, notably savings, accessible. Inefficient institutions, corruption and political instability can also discourage investment. Aid and government support in health, education and infrastructure helps growth by increasing human and physical capital.

CAUSES

Scarcity of Basic Needs

Before the industrial revolution, poverty had been mostly accepted as inevitable as economies produced little, making wealth scarce. In Antwerp and Lyon, two of the largest cities in western Europe, by 1600 three-quarters of the total population were too poor to pay taxes. In 18th century England, half the population was at least occasionally dependent on charity for subsistence. In modern times, food shortages have been reduced dramatically in the developed world, thanks to agricultural technologies such as nitrogen fertilisers, pesticides and new irrigation methods. Also, mass production of goods in places such as China has made what were once considered luxuries, such as vehicles or computers, inexpensive and thus accessible to many who were otherwise too poor to afford them.

Rises in the costs of living make poor people less able to afford items. Poor people spend a greater portion of their budgets on food than richer people. As a result poor households, and those near the poverty threshold can be particularly vulnerable to increases in food prices. For example in late 2007 increases in the price of grains led to food riots in some countries. The World Bank warned that 100 million people were at risk of sinking deeper into poverty. Threats to the supply of food may also be caused by drought and the water crisis. Intensive farming often leads to a vicious cycle of exhaustion of soil fertility and decline of agricultural yields. Approximately 40% of the world's agricultural land is seriously degraded. In Africa, if current trends of soil degradation continue, the continent might be able to feed just 25% of its population by 2025, according to UNU's Ghana-based Institute for Natural Resources in Africa.

Health care can be widely unavailable to the poor. The loss of health care workers emigrating from impoverished countries has a damaging effect. For example, an estimated 100,000 Philippine nurses emigrated between 1994 and 2006. There are more Ethiopian doctors in Chicago than in Ethiopia.

Overpopulation and lack of access to birth control methods drive poverty The world's population is expected to reach nearly 9 billion in 2040. However, the reverse is also true, that poverty causes overpopulation as it gives women little power to plan childhood, have educational attainment, or a career.

Barriers to Opportunities

The unwillingness of governments and feudal elates to give full-fledged property rights of land to their tenants is cited as the chief obstacle to development. This lack of economic freedom inhibits entrepreneurship among the poor. New enterprises and foreign investment can be driven away by the results of inefficient institutions, notably corruption, weak rule of law and excessive bureaucratic burdens. Lack of financial services, as a result of restrictive regulations, such as the requirements for banking licenses, makes it hard for even smaller micro-savings programs to reach the poor.

It takes two days, two bureaucratic procedures, and $280 to open a business in Canada while an entrepreneur in Bolivia must pay $2,696 in fees, wait 82 business days, and go through 20 procedures to do the same. Such costly barriers favour big firms at the expense of small enterprises, where most jobs are created. In India before economic reforms, businesses had to bribe government officials even for routine activities, which was a tax on business in effect.

Corruption, for example, in Nigeria, led to an estimated $400 billion of the country's oil revenue to be stolen by

Nigeria's leaders between 1960 and 1999. Lack of opportunities can further be caused by the failure of governments to provide essential infrastructure.

Opportunities in richer countries drives talent away, leading to brain drains. This is mainly caused by richer countries' restrictions on Freedom of Movement of the poor, uneducated class. Entry visas are granted with much higher probability to the rich and educated of developing countries. Brain drain has cost the African continent over $4 billion in the employment of 150,000 expatriate professionals annually. Indian students going abroad for their higher studies costs India a foreign exchange outflow of $10 billion annually.

Poor health and education severely affects productivity. Inadequate nutrition in childhood undermines the ability of individuals to develop their full capabilities. Lack of essential minerals such as iodine and iron can impair brain development. Two billion people (one-third of the total global population) are affected by iodine deficiency. In developing countries, it is estimated that 40% of children aged 4 and younger suffer from anaemia because of insufficient iron in their diets.

Similarly substancc abusc, including for example alcoholism and drug abuse can consign people to vicious poverty cycles. Infectious diseases such as Malaria and tuberculosis can perpetuate poverty by diverting health and economic resources from investment and productivity; malaria decreases GDP growth by up to 1.3% in some developing nations and AIDS decreases African growth by 0.3-1.5% annually.

War, political instability and crime, including violent gangs and drug cartels, also discourage investment. Civil wars and conflicts in Africa cost the continent some $300 billion between 1990 and 2005. Arteria and Ethiopia spent hundreds of millions of dollars on the war that resulted in minor border changes. Shocks in the business cycle affect poverty rates, increasing in recessions and declining in booms. Cultural factors, such as discrimination of various kinds, can negatively affect productivity such as age discrimination, stereotyping, gender discrimination, racial discrimination, and caste discrimination.

Max Weber and the modernisation theory suggest that cultural values could affect economic success. However, researchers have gathered evidence that suggest that values are not as deeply ingrained and that changing economic opportunities explain most of the movement into and out of poverty, as opposed to shifts in values.

Effects of Poverty

The effects of poverty may also be causes, as listed above, thus creating a "poverty cycle" operating across multiple levels, individual, local, national and global.

Health Problems

Hunger, disease, and less education describe a person in poverty. One third of deaths-some 18 million people a year or 50,000 per day-are due to poverty-related causes: in total 270 million people, most of them women and children, have died as a result of poverty since 1990. Those living in poverty suffer disproportionately from hunger or even starvation and disease. Those living in poverty suffer lower life expectancy. According to the World Health Organisation, hunger and malnutrition are the single gravest threats to the world's public health and malnutrition is by far the biggest contributor to child mortality, present in half of all cases.

Every year nearly 11 million children living in poverty die before their fifth birthday. 1.02 billion people go to bed hungry every night. Poverty increases the risk of homelessness. There are over 100 million street children worldwide. Increased risk of drug abuse may also be associated with poverty.

According to the Global Hunger Index, South Asia has the highest child malnutrition rate of the world's regions. Nearly half of all Indian children are undernourished, one of the highest rates in the world and nearly double the rate of Sub Saharan Africa. Every year, more than half a million women die in pregnancy or childbirth. Almost 90% of maternal deaths occur in Asia and sub-Saharan Africa, compared to less than 1% in the developed world.

Women who have children born in poverty cannot nourish the children efficiently with the right prenatal care. They may also suffer from disease that may be passed down to the child through birth. Asthma is a common problem children acquire when born into poverty.

Education

Research has found that there is a high risk of educational underachievement for children who are from low-income housing circumstances. This often is a process that begins in primary school for some less fortunate children. In the US educational system, these children are at a higher risk than other children for retention in their grade, special placements during the school's hours and even not completing their high school education. There are indeed many explanations for why students tend to drop out of school. For children with low resources, the risk factors are similar to excuses such as juvenile delinquency rates, higher levels of teenage pregnancy, and the economic dependency upon their low income parent or parents.

Families and society who submit low levels of investment in the education and development of less fortunate children end up with less favourable results for the children who see a life of parental employment reduction and low wages. Higher rates of early childbearing with all the connected risks to family, health and well-being are maturely important issues to address since education from preschool to high school are both identifiably meaningful in a life.

Poverty often drastically affects children's success in school. A child's "home activities, preferences, mannerisms" must align with the world and in the cases that they do not these students are at a disadvantage in the school and most importantly the classroom. Therefore, it is safe to state that children who live at or below the poverty level will have far less success educationally than children who live above the poverty line. Poor children have a great deal less health care and this ultimately results in many absences from the academic year. Additionally, poor children are much more likely to suffer from hunger, fatigue, irritability, headaches, ear infections, flu, and colds. These illnesses could potentially restrict a child or student's focus and concentration.

Housing

Slum-dwellers, who make up a third of the world's urban population, live in a poverty no better, if not worse, than rural people, who are the traditional focus of the poverty in the developing world, according to a report by the United Nations.

Most of the children living in institutions around the world have a surviving parent or close relative, and they most commonly entered orphanages because of poverty. Experts and child advocates maintain that orphanages are expensive and often harm children's development by separating them from their families. It is speculated that, flush with money, orphanages are increasing and push for children to join even though demographic data show that even the poorest extended families usually take in children whose parents have died.

Violence

According to a UN report on modern slavery, the most common form of human trafficking is for prostitution, which is largely fuelled by poverty. In Zimbabwe, a number of girls are turning to prostitution for food to survive because of the increasing poverty. In one survey, 67% of children from disadvantaged inner cities said they had witnessed a serious assault, and 33% reported witnessing a homicide. 51% of fifth graders from New Orleans have been found to be victims of violence, compared to 32% in Washington, DC.

Drug Abuse

Unemployment and distance from rural areas are where most drug abuse occurs. Drug abuse can result in a community shouldering the impact of many nefarious acts such as stealing, killing, theft, sexual assault, and prostitution. Drug abuse is synonymous with poor performance in school & work, and a general malaise of intra-personal intelligence. People who have abused drugs and have spent all of their money buying substances—i.e. heroin, alcohol, methamphetamine etc.—become addicts. This induces a downward spiral in the functionality of most addicts, as the drugs and poverty can be cyclical. When an addict has no other way to support their addiction they result to illegal measures to obtain income. This is where a community becomes affected by drug abuse.

Absolute Poverty

Poverty is usually measured as either absolute or relative poverty (the latter being actually an index of income inequality). Absolute poverty refers to a set standard which is consistent over time and between countries. The World Bank defines extreme poverty as living on less than US $1.25 (PPP) per day, and moderate poverty as less than $2 a day. It estimates that "in 2001, 1.1 billion people had consumption levels below $1 a day and 2.7 billion lived on less than $2 a day."

Six million children die of hunger every year - 17,000 every day. Selective Primary Health Care has been shown to be one of the most efficient ways in which absolute poverty can be eradicated in comparison to Primary Health Care which has a target of treating diseases. Disease prevention is the focus of Selective Primary Health Care which puts this system on higher grounds in terms of preventing malnutrition and illness, thus putting an end to Absolute Poverty.

The proportion of the developing world's population living in extreme economic poverty fell from 28 percent in 1990 to 21 percent in 2001. Most of this improvement has occurred in East and South Asia. In East Asia the World Bank reported that "The poverty headcount rate at the $2-a-day level is estimated to have fallen to about 27 percent, down from 29.5 percent in 2006 and 69 percent in 1990." In Sub-Saharan Africa extreme poverty went up from 41 percent in 1981 to 46 percent in 2001, which combined with growing population increased the number of people living in extreme poverty from 231 million to 318 million.

In the early 1990s some of the transition economies of Eastern Europe and Central Asia experienced a sharp drop in income. The collapse of the Soviet Union resulted in large declines in GDP per capita, of about 30 to 35% between 1990 and the trough year of 1998 (when it was at its minimum). As a result poverty rates also increased although in subsequent years as per capita incomes recovered the poverty rate dropped from 31.4% of the population to 19.6%. The World Bank issued a report predicting that between 2007 and 2027 the population of Georgia and Ukraine will decrease by 17% and 24% respectively.

World Bank data shows that the percentage of the population living in households with consumption or income per person below the poverty line has decreased in each region of the world since 1990:

Region	1990	2002	2004
East Asia and Pacific	15.40%	12.33%	9.07%
Europe and Central Asia	3.60%	1.28%	0.95%
Latin America and the Caribbean	9.62%	9.08%	8.64%
Middle East and North Africa	2.08%	1.69%	1.47%
South Asia	35.04%	33.44%	30.84%
Sub-Saharan Africa	46.07%	42.63%	41.09%

Other human development indicators have also been improving. Life expectancy has greatly increased in the developing world since WWII and is starting to close the gap to the developed world. Child mortality has decreased in every developing region of the world. The proportion of the world's population living in countries where per-capita food supplies are less than 2,200 calories per day decreased from 56% in the mid-1960s to below 10% by the 1990s. Similar trends can be observed for literacy, access to clean water and electricity and basic consumer items.

There are various criticisms of these measurements. Shaohua Chen and Martin Ravallion note that although "a clear trend decline in the percentage of people who are absolutely poor is evident... with uneven progress across regions... The developing world outside China and India has seen little or no sustained progress in reducing the number of poor".

Since the world's population is increasing, a constant number living in poverty would be associated with a diminishing proportion. Looking at the percentage living on less than $1/day, and if excluding China and India, then this percentage has decreased from 31.35% to 20.70% between 1981 and 2004.

The 2007 World Bank report "Global Economic Prospects" predicts that in 2030 the number living on less than the equivalent of $1 a day will fall by half, to about 550 million. An average resident of what we used to call the Third World will live about as well as do residents of the Czech or Solvate republics today. Much of Africa will have difficulty keeping pace with the rest of the developing world and even if conditions there improve in absolute terms, the report warns, Africa in 2030 will be home to a larger proportion of the world's poorest people than it is today.

The reason for the faster economic growth in East Asia and South Asia is a result of their relative backwardness, in a phenomenon called the convergence hypothesis or the conditional convergence hypothesis. Because these economies began modernising later than richer nations, they could benefit from simply adapting technological advances which enable higher levels of productivity that had been invented over centuries in richer nations.

Relative Poverty

Relative poverty views poverty as socially defined and dependent on social context, hence relative poverty is a measure of income inequality. Usually, relative poverty is measured as the percentage of population with income less than some fixed proportion of median income. There are several other different income inequality matrix, for example the Gini coefficient or the Theil -Index. Relative poverty measures are used as official poverty rates in several developed countries. As such these poverty statistics measure inequality rather than material deprivation or hardship. The measurements are usually based on a person's yearly income and frequently take no account of total wealth. The main poverty line used in the OECD and the European Union is based on "economic distance", a level of income set at 60% of the median household income.

Economic Aspects of Poverty

Economic aspects of poverty focus on material needs, typically including the necessities of daily living, such as food, clothing, shelter, or safe drinking water. Poverty in this sense may be understood as a condition in which a person or community is lacking in the basic needs for a minimum standard of well-being and life, particularly as a result of a persistent lack of income.

Analysis of social aspects of poverty links conditions of scarcity to aspects of the distribution of resources and power in a society and recognises that poverty may be a function of the diminished "capability" of people to live the kinds of lives they value. The social aspects of poverty may include lack of access to information, education, health care, or political power.

Poverty may also be understood as an aspect of unequal social status and inequitable social relationships, experienced as social exclusion, dependency, and diminished capacity to participate, or to develop meaningful connections with other people in society. Such social exclusion can be minimised through strengthened connections with the mainstream, such as through the provision of relational care to those who are experiencing poverty.

The World Bank's "Voices of the Poor," based on research with over 20,000 poor people in 23 countries, identifies a range of factors which poor people identify as part of poverty. These include:

— Precarious livelihoods.
— Excluded locations.
— Physical limitations.
— Gender relationships.
— Problems in social relationships.
— Lack of security.
— Abuse by those in power.
— Dis-empowering institutions.
— Limited capabilities.
— Weak community organisations.

David Moore, in his book The World Bank, argues that some analysis of poverty reflect pejorative, sometimes racial, stereotypes of impoverished people as powerless victims and passive recipients of aid programs.

Ultra-poverty, a term apparently coined by Michael Lipton, connotes being amongst poorest of the poor in low-income countries. Lipton defined ultra-poverty as receiving less than 80 percent of minimum caloric intake whilst spending more than 80% of income on food. Alternatively a 2007 report issued by International Food Policy Research Institute defined ultra-poverty as living on less than 54 cents per day. BRAC (NGO) has pioneered a program called Targeting the Ultra-Poor to redress ultra-poverty by working with individual ultra-poor women.

Voluntary Poverty

Among some individuals, such as ascetics, poverty is considered a necessary or desirable condition, which must be embraced in order to reach certain spiritual, moral, or intellectual states. Poverty is often understood to be an essential element of renunciation in religions such as Buddhism (only for monks, not for lay persons) and Jainism, whilst in Roman Catholicism it is one of the evangelical counsels.

Certain religious orders also take a vow of extreme poverty. For example, the Franciscan orders have traditionally foregone all individual and corporate forms of ownership. While individual ownership of goods and wealth is forbidden for Benedictines, following the Rule of St. Benedict, the monastery itself may possess both goods and money, and throughout history some monasteries have become very rich.

In this context of religious vows, poverty may be understood as a means of self-denial in order to place oneself at the service of others; Pope Honorius III wrote in 1217 that the Dominicans "lived a life of voluntary poverty, exposing themselves to innumerable dangers and suffering, for the salvation of others". Following Jesus' warning that riches can be like thorns that choke up the good seed of the word, voluntary poverty is often understood by Christians as of benefit to the individual–a form of self-discipline by which one distances oneself from distractions from God.

Poverty Reduction

Poverty has historically been accepted as inevitable as non-industrialised economies produced very little while population grew almost as fast making wealth scarce. Poverty reduction, or poverty alleviation, has been largely as a result of overall economic growth. Food shortages were common before modern agricultural technology and in places that lack them today, such as nitrogen fertilisers, pesticides and irrigation methods. The dawn of industrial revolution led to high economic growth, eliminating mass poverty in what is now considered the developed world. World GDP per person quintupled during the 20th century. In 1820, 75% of humanity lived on less than a dollar a day, while in 2001, only about 20% do. Today, continued economic development is constrained by the lack of economic freedom. Economic liberalisation requires extending property rights to the poor, especially to land. Financial services, notably savings, can be made accessible to the poor through technology, such as mobile banking. Inefficient institutions, corruption and political instability can also discourage investment. Aid and government support in health, education and infrastructure helps growth by increasing human and physical capital.

Poverty alleviation also involves improving the living conditions of people who are already poor. Aid, particularly in medical and scientific areas, is essential in providing better lives, such as the green revolution and the eradication of smallpox. Problems with today's development aid include the high proportion of tied aid, which mandates receiving nations to buy products, often more expensive, originating only from donor countries. Nevertheless, some believe that small changes in the way each of us in affluent nations lives our lives could solve world poverty.

Economic Liberalisation

Extending property rights protection to the poor is one of the most important poverty reduction strategy a nation could take. Securing property rights to land, the largest asset for most societies, is vital to their economic freedom. The World Bank concludes increasing land rights is 'the key to reducing poverty' citing that land rights greatly increase poor people's wealth, in some cases doubling it. It is estimated that state recognition of the property of the poor would give them assets worth 40 times all the foreign aid since 1945. Although approaches varied, the World Bank said the key issues were security of tenure and ensuring land transactions were low cost. In China and India, noted reductions in poverty in recent decades have occurred mostly as a result of the abandonment of collective farming in China and the cutting of government red tape in India.

New enterprises and foreign investment can be driven away by the results of inefficient institutions, notably corruption, weak rule of law and excessive bureaucratic burdens. It takes two days, two bureaucratic procedures, and \$280 to open a business in Canada while an entrepreneur in Bolivia must pay \$2,696 in fees, wait 82 business days, and go through 20 procedures to do the same. Such costly barriers favour big firms at the expense of small enterprises, where most jobs are created. In India before economic reforms, businesses had to bribe government officials even for routine activities, which was a tax on business in effect.

However, ending government sponsorship of social programs is sometimes advocated as a free market principle with tragic consequences. For example, the World Bank presses poor nations to eliminate subsidies for fertiliser even while many farmers cannot afford them at market prices. The re-configuration of public financing in former Soviet states during their transition to a market economy called for reduced spending on health and education, sharply increasing poverty.

Trade liberalisation increases total surplus of trading nations. Remittances sent to poor countries, such as India, are sometimes larger than foreign direct investment and total remittances are more than double aid flows from OECD countries. Foreign investment and export industries helped fuel the economic expansion of fast growing Asian nations. However, trade rules are often unfair as they block access to richer nations' markets and ban poorer nations from supporting their industries. Processed products from poorer nations, in contrast to raw materials, get vastly higher tariffs at richer nations' ports.

A University of Toronto study found the dropping of duty charges on thousands of products from African nations because of the African Growth and Opportunity Act was directly responsible for a "surprisingly large" increase in imports from Africa. Deals can sometimes be negotiated to favour the developing country such as in China, where laws compel foreign multinationals to train their future Chinese competitors in strategic industries and render themselves redundant in the long term. In Thailand, the 51 percent rule compels multinational corporations starting operations in Thailand give 51 percent control to a Thai company in a joint venture.

Capital, Infrastructure and Technology

Long run economic growth per person is achieved through increases in capital (factors that increase productivity), both human and physical, and technology. Improving human capital; in the form of health, is needed for economic growth. Nations do not necessarily need wealth to gain health. For example, Sri Lanka had a maternal mortality rate of 2% in the 1930s, higher than any nation today. It reduced it to.5-.6% in the 1950s and to.06% today. However, it was spending less each year on maternal health because it learned what worked and what did not. Knowledge on the cost effectiveness of health care interventions can be elusive but educational measures to disseminate what works are available, such as the disease control priorities project. Promoting hand washing is one of the most cost effective health intervention and can cut deaths from the major childhood diseases of diarrhoea and pneumonia by half.

Human capital, in the form of education, is an even more important determinant of economic growth than physical capital. De-worming children costs about 50 cents per child per year and reduces non-attendance from anaemia, illness and malnutrition and is only a twenty-fifth as expensive to increase school attendance as by constructing schools.

UN economists argue that good infrastructure, such as roads and information networks, helps market reforms to work. China claims it is investing in railways, roads, ports and rural telephones in African countries as part of its formula for economic development. It was the technology of the steam engine that originally began the dramatic decreases in poverty levels. Cell phone technology brings the market to poor or rural sections. With necessary information, remote farmers can produce specific crops to sell to the buyers that brings the best price.

Such technology also helps bring economic freedom by making financial services accessible to the poor. Those in poverty place overwhelming importance on having a safe place to save money, much more so than receiving loans. Also, a large part of micro-finance loans are spent on products that would usually be paid by a checking or savings account. Mobile banking addresses the problem of the heavy regulation and costly maintenance of saving accounts. Mobile financial services in the developing world, ahead of the developed world in this respect, could be worth $5 billion by 2012. Safaricom's M-Pesa launched one of the first systems where a network of agents of mostly shopkeepers, instead of bank branches, would take deposits in cash and translate these onto a virtual account on customers' phones. Cash transfers can be done between phones and issued back in cash with a small commission, making remittances safer.

Aids

Welfare Aids

Aid in its simplest form is a basic income grant, a form of social security periodically providing citizens with money. In pilot projects in Namibia, where such a program pays just $13 a month, people were able to pay tuition fees, raising the proportion of children going to school by 92%, child malnutrition rates fell from 42% to 10% and economic activity grew 10%. Aid could also be rewarded based on doing certain requirements.

Conditional Cash Transfers, widely credited as a successful anti-poverty program, is based on actions such as enrolling children in school or receiving vaccinations. In Mexico, for example, the country with the largest such program, dropout rates of 16-19 year old in rural area dropped by 20% and children gained half an inch in height. Initial fears that the program would encourage families to stay at home rather than work to collect benefits have proven to be unfounded. Instead, there is less excuse for neglectful behaviour as, for example, children are prevented from begging on the streets instead of going to school because it could result in suspension from the program.

Welfare states have an effect on poverty reduction. Currently modern, expansive welfare states that ensure economic opportunity, independence and security in a near universal manner are still the exclusive domain of the developed nations. Commonly constituting at least 20% of GDP, with the largest Scandinavia welfare states constituting over 40% of GDP. These modern welfare states, which largely arose in the late 19th and early 20th centuries, seeing their greatest expansion in the mid 20th century, and have proven themselves highly effective in reducing relative as well as absolute poverty in all analysed high-income OECD countries.

Development Aid

A major proportion of aid from donor nations is 'tied', mandating that a receiving nation buy products originating only from the donor country. This can be harmful economically. For example, Arteria is forced to spend aid money on foreign goods and services to build a network of railways even though it is cheaper to use local expertise and resources. Money from the United States to fight AIDS requires it be spent on U.S brand name drugs that can cost up to $15,000 a year compared to $350 a year for generics from other countries. Only Norway, Denmark, Netherlands and Britain have stopped tying their aid.

Some think tanks and NGOs have argued that Western monetary aid often only serves to increase poverty and social inequality, either because it is conditioned with the implementation of harmful economic policies in the recipient countries, or because it's tied with the importing of products from the donor country over cheaper alternatives, or because foreign aid is seen to be serving the interests of the donor more than the recipient. Critics also argue that some of the foreign aid is stolen by corrupt governments and officials, and that higher aid levels erode the quality of governance.

Policy becomes much more oriented toward what will get more aid money than it does towards meeting the needs of the people. Problems with the aid system and not aid itself are that the aid is excessively directed towards the salaries of consultants from donor countries, the aid is not spread properly, neglecting vital, less publicised area such as agriculture, and the aid is not properly coordinated among donors, leading to a plethora of disconnected projects rather than unified strategies.

Supporters of aid argue that these problems may be solved with better auditing of how the aid is used. Immunisation campaigns for children, such as against polio, diphtheria and measles have save millions of lives. Aid from non-governmental organisations may be more effective than governmental aid; this may be because it is better at reaching the poor and better controlled at the grassroots level. As a point of comparison, the annual world military spending is over $1 trillion.

Debt Relief

One of the proposed ways to help poor countries that emerged during the 1980's has been debt relief. Given that many less developed nations have gotten themselves into extensive debt to banks and governments from the rich nations, and given that the interest payments on these debts are often more than a country can generate per year in profits from exports, cancelling part or all of these debts may allow poor nations "to get out of the hole". If poor countries do not have to spend so much on debt payments, they can use the money instead for priorities which help reduce poverty such as basic health-care and education. Many nations began offering services, such as free health care even while overwhelming the health care infrastructure, because of savings that resulted from the rounds of debt relief in 2005.

Role of Education and Skill-building

Universal public education has some role in preparing youth for basic academic skills and perhaps many trade skills, as well. Apprenticeships clearly build needed trade skills. If modest amounts of cash and land can be combined with a modicum of agricultural skills in a temperate climate, subsistence can give way toward modest socialite wealth. As has been mentioned, education for women will allow for reduced family size—an important poverty reduction event in its own right.

While all components mentioned above are necessary, the portion of education pertaining to the variety of skills needed to build and maintain the infrastructure of a developing (moving out of poverty) society: building trades; plumbing; electrician; well-drilling; farm and transport mechanical skills (and others) are clearly needed in large numbers of individuals, if the society is to move out of poverty or subsistence. Yet, many well-developed western economies are moving strongly away from the essential apprenticeships and skill training which affords a clear vocational path out of modern urban poverty.

Micro-loans

One of the most popular of the new technical tools for economic development and poverty reduction are Micro-loans made famous in 1976 by the Grameen Bank in Bangladesh. The idea is to loan small amounts of money to farmers or villages so these people can obtain the things they need to increase their economic rewards. A small pump costing only $50 could make a very big difference in a village without the means of irrigation, for example. A couple of hundred dollars for a small bridge linking a village to a city where it can market farm products is another example. A specific example is the Thai government's People's Bank which is making loans of $100 to $300 to help farmers buy equipment or seeds, help street vendors acquire an inventory to sell, or help others set up small shops.

Micro-enterprise Development adds teaching of basic financial principles and general business training before providing loan capital, thus is very practical and sound approach to fighting poverty. This approach is advocated by Five Talents as the way to ensure that entrepreneurs and their communities benefit now and in the future with documented success stories

Good Institutions

Efficient institutions that are not corrupt and obey the rule of law make and enforce good laws that provide security to property and businesses. Efficient and fair governments would work to invest in the long-term interests of the nation rather than plunder resources through corruption.

Researchers at UC Berkely developed what they called a "Weberianness scale" which measures aspects of bureaucracies and governments Max Weber described as most important for rational-legal and efficient government over 100 years ago. Comparative research has found that the scale is correlated with higher rates of economic development. With their related concept of good governance World Bank researchers have found much the same: Data from 150 nations have shown several measures of good governance (such as accountability, effectiveness, rule of law, low corruption) to be related to higher rates of economic development.

Funds from aid and natural resources are often diverted into private hands and then sent to banks overseas as a result of graft. If Western banks rejected stolen money, says a report by Global Witness, ordinary people would benefit "in a way that aid flows will never achieve". The report asked for more regulation of banks as they have proved capable of stanching the flow of funds linked to terrorism, money-laundering or tax evasion.

Examples of good governance leading to economic development and poverty reduction include Thailand, Taiwan, Malaysia, South Korea, and Vietnam, which tend to have a strong government, called a hard state or development state. These "hard states" have the will and authority to create and maintain policies that lead to long-term development that helps all their citizens, not just the wealthy. Multinational corporations are regulated so that they follow reasonable standards for pay and labour conditions, pay reasonable taxes to help develop the country, and keep some of the profits in the country, reinvesting them to provide further development.

The United Nations Development Program published a report in April 2000 which focused on good governance in poor countries as a key to economic development and overcoming the selfish interests of wealthy elates often behind state actions in developing nations. The report concludes that "Without good governance, reliance on trickle-down economic development and a host of other strategies will not work." Despite the promise of such research several questions remain, such as where good governance comes from and how it can be achieved. The comparative analysis of one sociologist suggests that broad historical forces have shaped the likelihood of good governance.

Ancient civilisations with more developed government organisation before colonialism, as well as elite responsibility, have helped create strong states with the means and efficiency to carry out development policies today. On the other hand strong states are not always the form of political organisation most conducive to economic development. Other historical factors, especially the experiences of colonialism for each country, have intervened to make a strong state and/or good governance less likely for some countries, especially in Africa. Another important factor that has been found to affect the quality of institutions and governance was the pattern of colonisation (how it took place) and even the identity of colonising power. International agencies may be able to promote good governance through various policies of intervention in developing nations as indicated in a few African countries, but comparative analysis suggests it may be much more difficult to achieve in most poor nations around the world.

Other Approaches

The role of women in poverty have also contributed to the cause of household survival. Thus, poverty reduction can only be actively done by understanding the level of gender role and gender differences within households. This will help reduce factors of poverty aside from the obvious income disparities. When given more rights and opportunities women begin to receive more education, thus increasing the overall human capital of the country; when given more influence women seem to act more responsibly in helping people in the family or village; and when better educated and more in control of their lives, women are more successful in bringing down rapid population growth because they have more say in family planning.

Another approach that has been proposed for alleviating poverty is Fair Trade which advocates the payment of an above market price as well as social and environmental standards in areas related to the production of goods. The efficacy of this approach to poverty reduction is controversial.

Community and monetary economist Thomas H. Greco, Jr. has argued that the mainstream global economy with its debt-based currency has built-in structural incentives that create poverty through keeping money scarce. Greco points to the success of modern barter clubs and historical local currencies such as the Wörgl Experiment at revitalising stagnant local economies, and calls for the creation of community currency as a means to reduce or eliminate poverty.

The Toronto Dollar is an example of a local currency oriented towards reducing poverty. Toronto Dollars are sold and redeemed in such a way that raise funds which are then given as grants to local charities, primarily ones oriented towards reducing poverty. Toronto Dollars also provide a means to create an incentive for welfare recipients to work: Toronto dollars can be given as gifts to welfare recipients who perform volunteer work for charitable and non-profit organisations, and these gifts do not affect welfare benefits.

Some have argued for radical economic change in the system. There are several fundamental proposals for restructuring existing economic relations, and many of their supporters argue that their ideas would reduce or even eliminate poverty entirely if they were implemented. Such proposals have been put forward by both left-wing and right-wing groups: socialism, communism, anarchism, libertarianism, binary economics and participatory economics, among others.

Inequality can be reduced by progressive taxation, wealth tax, and inheritance tax. In law, there has been a move to establish the absence of poverty as a human right. The IMF and member countries have produced Poverty Reduction Strategy papers or PRSPs. In his book" The End of Poverty", a prominent economist named Jeffrey Sacks laid out a plan to eradicate global poverty by the year 2025. Following his recommendations, international organisations such as the Global Solidarity Network are working to help eradicate poverty worldwide with intervention in the areas of housing, food, education, basic health, agricultural inputs, safe drinking water, transportation and communications.

The Poor People's Economic Human Rights Campaign is an organisation in the United States working to secure freedom from poverty for all by organising the poor themselves. The Campaign believes that a human rights framework, based on the value of inherent dignity and worth of all persons, offers the best means by which to organise for a political solution to poverty.

3

Inequality and Social Conflicts

The links between inequality and violent conflict is one of the oldest concerns of political economy. "We maintain that if a state is to avoid the greatest plague of all—I mean civil war, though civil disintegration would be a better term—extreme poverty and wealth must not be allowed to arise in any section of the citizen-body, because both lead to both these disasters". It is almost a universal assumption that an inequitable distribution of resources and wealth will provoke violent rebellion.

For example, in 1562 Montaigne met a small group of Indians from Brazil (the subject of his essay, On Cannibals) and asked them what they found most remarkable about their visit to France. One of the answers was that they had noticed among us some men gorged to the full with things of every sort while their other halves were beggars at their doors, emaciated with hunger and poverty. They found it strange that these poverty-stricken halves [sic] should suffer such injustice, and that they did not take the others by the throat or set fire to their houses

And yet it is just as obvious and historically established that sharply skewed income and wealth distribution does not always or even usually lead to rebellion. This is generally taken to mean that the inequality is legitimised in one way or another; that the inequality comes with a degree of power and repression that are simply too great to overcome; or that there are various obstacles preventing collective action.

Inequality in some form or other is a constant of all hierarchical social order. Violence too is prevalent in human society. However, while organised violent political conflict ebbs and flows; it is interspersed with periods of peace. Thus:

— Inequality may not be a cause of conflict and may not perhaps be necessary or sufficient for violent conflict;

— Some characteristics of this inequality, rather than inequality itself, may be more relevant; and

— Perhaps something in the intensity of inequality, measured in various ways (including but not limited to the Gini coefficient may be relevant to the outbreak of violent conflict (implying a threshold that itself may vary with social, political and cultural conditions as well as with the average level of income).

Studying inequality usually involves the study of symptoms and outcomes. This is especially true of large sample quantitative studies of the links between inequality and political conflict. However, to understand the links from inequality to conflict (if they exist), rather than just trying to identify statistical patterns of event regularity, we need to study what produces and underpins inequality and how this might relate to conflict. This is all the more necessary if large sample quantitative studies do not generate unequivocal results.

Yet the long history of interest in the links between inequality and violent conflict has not been matched by an evolving progression in theory or empirical certainty. Lichbach frets over the lack of theoretical progress. And Cramer argues that empirically there remains huge indeterminacy in this discussion of linkages between economic inequality and violent political conflict. One of the more recent trends in thinking about violent conflict has been the ascendancy of neoclassical economic analysis and modelling. Much of this eschews reference to earlier studies, as though work in other disciplines were a territory without history. However, there is really little, if anything, new in this neoclassical economic explanation of violent conflict. Most of the explanations have been put forward in earlier rational choice, methodologically individualist work.

Research on Conflict and Inequality

There are various ways of distinguishing among theories of violent conflict at a general theoretical level: that is, distinguishing what kind of theoretical tradition they spring from. This section briefly characterises a few of these schema and general forms of theoretical framework for explaining violent political conflict. The set of approaches highlighted might not be exhaustive but does capture most of the range as well as illustrating a dynamic aspect of the question, such as how various theoretical approaches have fared during the past 20 or 30 years.

The discussion makes one broad illustrative point. A comparison of these frameworks shows that claims about the link from inequality to violent political conflict may reflect more than one analytical approach. Overlapping claims about an inequality-conflict relationship may contain contrasting theories of the mechanisms by which inequality "translates" into violent conflict. This review partly hopes to disentangle these claims. It also hopes to highlight the enduring imprecision in most discussions of what Lichbach called the "economic inequality–political conflict (EI-PC) nexus".

Since the literature on inequality and conflict is generally located within the political economy of development, the discussion is restricted to conflict theories that have an obvious bearing on or source in this development field, including development economics, new growth theory, historical political economy and political science. Among various possible ways of organising and classifying theories of conflict (particularly "internal war", "intrastate conflict" or "civil war"), three are particularly useful.

One of these divides all such theories at a "branch point" where a fundamental choice of perspective is made: between contingency and inherence. A second distinguishes between "deprived-actor" theories and "rational-actor" theories. A third cuts the pack three ways: into theories, or stories, emphasising behaviour, ideas or relations. However, this section also briefly highlights neoclassical economic theories of violent conflict. These theories have become increasingly popular and, in some circles, influential since the mid-1990s. Although representing one strand of rational-actor theory, orthodox economic theories or models themselves are somewhat inconsistent and allow for varying distributional arguments.

The image of a territorial encounter, between disciplines, is appropriate for a field in which some claim argued that all theories of conflict priorities at a fundamental level either the significance of contingency in unleashing collective violence or that of inherent propensities to violence. Collective violence driven by contingency is, according to this framework, largely affective, though this does not rule out some purposive, rational influence. By contrast, theories stressing an inherent disposition toward collective violence emphasise rational calculation over "irrational", affective outbursts.

From the perspective of contingency, war and other forms of collective violence are rarities or abnormal; and they are produced by extraordinary circumstances that work, typically, through what has been called the "frustration-aggression" nexus. Processes of development are responsible for eruptions of collective violence since they cut people loose from their "traditional" moorings (and mores), producing extreme frustrations, while the formation of new political institutions, which might manage the consequences of frustration, often flag behind. A range of mediating factors, secondary but still significant, and the locus of contingency, are necessary prompters of violence: cultures of violence, perhaps; ideological provocations; and/or the balance of coercive powers.

The most renowned, and still influential, example of this kind of theory about collective violence was Gurr's relative deprivation theory. Relative deprivation captured people's "perceptions of discrepancy between their value expectations (the goods and conditions of the life to which they believe they are justifiably entitled) and their value capabilities (the amounts of those goods and conditions that they think they are able to get and keep)". Note that this is a tension akin to Gerschenkron's in late industrialising nations between the promise of the benefits of industrialisation and the obstacles blocking the way to reaping those benefits. Thus, for Gurr, relative deprivation was likely to increase during the early stages of development, producing frustration and a socially unusual proclivity to aggression that might materialise into actual collective violence, given the specific constellation of (contingent) mediating factors. Gurr and Duvall formulated the link to political violence thus:

Magnitude of political violence = RD + (RD x JUST x BALANCE) + e where RD is relative deprivation, JUST is justification (beliefs, traditions), BALANCE captures the distribution of coercive and institution resources of dissidents versus the state, and e is an error term. This formulation neatly captured the mediating role of balance and justification. "Justification" has been sustained in the literature, for example, the recent emphasis on "perception" of grievance, inequality and so on, rather than on their objective presence only as an important determinant of conflict.

So-called inherency theories do not presume that collective violence is produced by aberrant conditions or rare combinations of extraordinary forces. Rather, they rest on an assumption that violence is an ever-present, entirely normal disposition in political life: violence is just one stretch of a continuum of collective action encompassing a range of forms of political competition. And violence, or nonviolence, is picked out from this continuum of options on the basis of rational calculation.

Processes of development may or may not present cost-benefit judgements that favour collective violence. Eckstein pictured this kind of analysis in terms of collective action theory. Thus, political life is dominated by interest groups vying for power. Nonmembers of some core ruling alliance of interests would make claims, demanding entry or recompense for claims made upon them. Depending on the reaction of the core group, this conflict of interests might lead to violence, for example, around "multiple sovereignty" claims.

Especially important in this model is the balance of coercive power and resources between groups. For it is precisely on the basis of this balance that groups will calculate the utility of war. Given that tactical choice based on objective indicators matters more than "virulent affect" in inherency theories, cultural traditions and social memory matter far less than in contingency theories. Nonetheless, it is still unclear why collective violence is not more common, from this perspective; and the answer will to some extent be driven by contingencies, accidents of history affecting facilitating factors and the coercive balance.

Another review of the inequality-conflict linkage argues for a fundamental division between analytical frameworks or "scientific research programmes" (SRPs) in terms of the deprived-actor/rational-actor distinction. Deprived-actor explanations stress the role of preferences, beliefs, values, hearts and minds. People form expectations, but in deprived-actor stories these are formed relative to other people's attributes, experience or performance. Rational-actor stories, on the other hand, assume that expectations and objectives are identified not relative to others but in self-referential processes. And decisions are taken largely in calculating terms: choices are made, based on cost-benefit judgements, and the keys lie in resources and opportunities more than beliefs.

Eckstein associates inherency theory especially with the work of Tilly on state formation and war, particularly in early modern Europe; and Lichbach identifies Tilly as a particular critic of the deprived-actor theory. In Tilly's work, with its focus on the politics of resource mobilisation, challengers make claims that are incompatible with the survival of the state in its existing form. These claims gather legitimacy when the state alienates significant groups of people by its failure to meet obligations or make reciprocal transfers to balance its own claims (taxes, levies) upon the population. If the central power cannot or will not effectively block the scope for extreme action, there is then a moment of multiple sovereignty in which mutually exclusive claims generate violence. Collective violence, in this kind of scenario, is a function of a lack of power, that is, where constraints on an inherent disposition toward violence are not effectively blocked.

Tilly himself has produced an alternative schema for distinguishing between theories of violent conflict. Thus, there are ideas theories, behaviour theories and relations theories of violence. For the purposes of this chapter, it is important only to note the following. First, Tilly observes that many explanations of social and political violence involve combinations of at least two of these underlying theoretical perspectives. Second, this analytical schema suggests a further distinction. For while Tilly is viewed as a member of the rational-actor, inherency-theory camp, this camp itself is not harmonious.

Tilly's work is clearly "relational" compared, for example, to neoclassical economic theories of conflict that are also very much rational-actor stories. Third, and related to this, there are different versions of what constitutes rationality. Neoclassical economic theory is based on methodological individualism and rational choice, in which rationality is basically non-relational and is tied to specific maximising utilitarian goals. However, there are other theories of rationality that priorities relational rationality and a wider range of goals influencing rational calculation. Further, an analysis may be influenced strongly by rational-actor assumptions but not be methodologically individualist.

In recent years, neoclassical economics has escaped its own confines and addressed a far wider range of social phenomena than before, including collective violence and war. According to some, there has been a period of "economics imperialism", as both its detractors and champions call it, and the analytical tools and fundamental axioms of neoclassical economics have come to dominate the social sciences in general. Certainly, neoclassical economics has had increasing influence on the study of violent conflict in developing countries in recent years. This has been driven especially by the theoretical work of Hirshleifer among others, and by the empirical models and policy work of Collier and his colleagues. Cramer provides a critique of this literature.

One apparent inconsistency in Collier—or, alternatively, one source of overlap between contingency and inherency theories—is that he claims to look for the rare but his assumptions, which, given his models, really derive theoretically from Hirshleifer, are that violence is a constant possibility, an option available to choice-making individuals. Arguably, the root of this ambiguity lies in an assumption that normality contains market perfection, since this is, after all, the benchmark against which he judges opportunities for violence to spring from market "distortion", suggesting that capitalism itself is naturally pacific. Keynes too assumed that economic activity and capitalism would overcome a fundamental disposition to violence, turning interests against passions.

Recent work by neoclassical economists has also created an analytical distinction between greed and grievance as alternative sources of civil war. This distinction also affects judgements of the role of inequality in the origins of wars. The greed and grievance distinction has achieved a fairly widespread influence. Although proponents of this distinction do not couch their analysis explicitly in these terms, grievance echoes "affective" outbursts of violence generated from the frustration-aggression nexus, while greed reflects cool calculating rationality associated with the inherency theory.

Inequality may have a role in more than one of these analytical perspectives. At first sight, though, inequality fits most neatly into a tradition of Eckstein's contingency theories, or Collier's (rejected) "grievance-based war. Inequality as a source of conflict is not precisely equivalent to relative deprivation. For relative deprivation focuses on the frustration engendered by current deprivation relative not necessarily to others within a polity but to what people perceive as justifiable.

A society could have a fairly even distribution of goods, assets and even opportunities but still fail to live up to people's perceptions, which no doubt would cause widespread frustration. Nonetheless, various indicators of inequality within a society may be a fair proxy for relative deprivation, since it would seem to justify grounds for frustration relative to those doing well in that society. Inequality, in other words, is likely to reveal or provoke a sense of relative deprivation. Nafziger and Auvinen make the link explicit, arguing that relative deprivation "often results from vertical (class) or horizontal (regional or communal) inequality".

The important implication of relative deprivation theory, however, is that inequality itself, and even perceived relative deprivation, will not cause violence without other mediating factors, notably "justification". That justification may come from "culture". However, another possibility, more awkward to contain within Eckstein's schema, is that justification may come from political and economic process and social relations. At one extreme, it is argued by Grinner that inequality, relative deprivation and grievous social conditions are a constant in most societies and that, therefore, the significance of "ideological moments" is more than just a secondary factor. Grinner argues that the incidence of collective violence in Central America ebbs and flows with the influence of particular ideologies of various times such as, for example, at one stage the communist revolutionary ideas affecting Central American intellectuals in the aftermath of the Cuban Revolution and, at another stage, the influence of liberal democratic ideology. In this kind of story, the contingency of external ideological influence is elevated to a central role, fitting nicely in Tilly's "ideas" category of theories of violent conflict. For Stewart), relative deprivation, to cause violent conflict, must have an objective and subjective base in horizontal inequality, that is, unequal distribution along regional, religious or ethnic lines. The point here is that violence will emerge from collective action among competitive groups, mobilising people around collective identity. Again, in this kind of story the brick wall dividing collective action from relative deprivation theories, or inherency from contingency theories, disintegrates.

Indeed, a priori there is nothing in most assumptions that inequality causes conflict that forces a fundamental choice between whether human society has an inherent, ever-present disposition toward collective violence and whether society is fundamentally peaceable. Nor is there a predetermined choice of whether—in violence potentially caused by inequality—violence is rational or affective. Inequality, therefore, may play a role both in theories that stress one or the other, or a combination of the two.

What Claims Have Been Made About the Relationship Between Inequality and Conflict?

It is perhaps not surprising that the politically most unstable nations are often characterised by market inequities. One approach to the problem has been to look for observable event regularities on the basis of multi-country samples, usually testing cross-sectional distributional data against the incidence of various forms of collective violence, including civil wars, protests, political murders and unconstitutional regime changes, and the one more recently in vogue, complex humanitarian emergencies (CHEs).

Distribution in these studies tends to be captured through either the income or the land Gini coefficients. A number of such studies did claim earlier to find some correlation but differed according to whether the data and their testing supported either a linear or a curvilinear relationship between distribution and collective violence. Thus Russett (found evidence of a linear relationship in a study relating the Gini coefficient of land distribution to a cumulative score of violent political deaths per million between 1950 and 1962. On the other hand, Nagel argued for a curvilinear relationship, in this case starting from data from different provinces in Vietnam but also looking at a wider sample of cases.

The curvilinear relationship takes the form of an inverted U shape: discontent begins at zero in an egalitarian society and increases up to some threshold level, beyond which discontent then tails off again as extreme inequality is approached. The argument would be that comparison is more odious where the difference between one person and a chosen comparator is fairly small, but that as this difference increases the tendency to compare oneself enviously, and hence to be locked into the frustration-aggression nexus, diminishes. Zimmerman summarising his own review of the literature on inequality, among other macro-statistical variables, argues:

> "Altogether, the limited empirical evidence available suggests a linear positive relationship between socioeconomic inequality and political violence".

He cautions, nonetheless, that the data and selection methods in sampling undermine confidence in most such studies and highlights the weaknesses in relying on cross-sectional rather than longitudinal datasets.

Recent proponents of the argument that economic inequality brings about violent political conflict and instability include Muller and Nafziger and Auvinen. Muller puts the argument in the context of debates over the relationship between development and democratisation. While a rising level of income per capita might well be a nurturing source of democratisation, largely because of the changes in the class composition and balance of society, Muller argues, there is typically a counter-vailing tendency insofar as rising levels of income usually imply increasing inequality in the distribution of income.

This is because "a high level of income inequality radicalism the working class, enhances class polarisation, and reduces the tolerance of the bourgeoisie for political participation by the lower classes". Muller cites his own cross-national study of 33 countries that showed a correlation between income inequality and the binary variable of stability versus instability of democracy between 1960 and 1980. Nafziger and Auvinen list high-income inequality along with stagnation and decline in real gross domestic product (GDP), a high ratio of military expenditures to national income, and a tradition of violent conflict as the main sources of humanitarian emergencies.

Large income inequality exacerbates the vulnerability of population to humanitarian emergencies. Nafziger and Auvinen use a Gini coefficient measure of inequality, applied to data from Deininger and Squire widely seen as the most reliable available data on inequality. This analysis explicitly claims that the evidence supports "objective grievances" contributing to war and humanitarian emergencies. The analysis also moves from a Gini coefficient measure of inequality to case study evidence of regional and ethnic, or "horizontal" inequalities arising from government discrimination.

There is also an argument from an orthodox economic perspective, stating that one of the reasons why inequality is bad for growth is that it provokes political instability and conflict. Nafziger and Auvinen cite in support the work of Alesina and Perotic whose cross-section study of 71 developing countries found that income inequality was associated with social discontent and sociopolitical instability (measured, for example, by the incidence of political assassinations), which in turn are correlated with lower investment.

Thus, inequality has of late been folded into the endogenous growth literature. In this literature, there are three main mechanisms by which inequality harms growth. First, inequality perpetuates a distorted human capital market, mis-allocating resources over time so that the wealthy over invest in the education of their offspring and the poor under invest. Suboptimal human capital investment then feeds into lower growth. Second, income inequality works on growth rates through a democratic political mechanism.

Thus, where inequality is high, the "median voter" may be expected to vote for redistributed taxes which, in turn, will reduce the return to investment and therefore act as a disincentive to capital. Third, inequality may reduce growth rates by deterring investment through political instability or war. Such claims are backed up by the literature on income inequality, human and "social" capital, and violent crime. Fajnzylber et al. Hsieh and Pugh all find in cross-sectional studies that increasing income inequality raises violent crime rates, while Wilson and Daly argue that life expectancy itself may be a psychosocial determinant of risk-taking behaviour, but that including in the model a measure of economic inequality adds significant extra predictive power. If Alesina and Perotti, Muller, Nafziger and Auvinen, and others subscribe implicitly to the linear relationship thesis, other work, mainly in the form of case studies, takes forward the idea of a curvilinear relationship.

However, curvilinear relationships come in two basic varieties, each mirroring the other exactly—one taking a U shape and the other an inverted U shape. A U-shaped relationship, in which (possibly for each level of income) there is some optimal distribution that minimises conflict, holds that either an increase or a decrease from this middle range of inequality will disturb the social peace. It might be in this middle range of inequality that Hirschman's "tolerance for inequality" dominates), according to which some people, observing the incomes of others pulling away from their own, interpret this as a signal of social mobility and patiently await a turn for the better in their own fortunes.

However, at higher degrees of inequality this effect would break down, as many people severed their own expectations from those of the beneficiaries of a higher Gini coefficient. And lower levels of inequality might reflect stagnant hopes and a free-for-all. By contrast, an inverted U curve would trace a pattern in which rising inequality (across or within societies) is associated first with increasing violent conflict and then, when inequality has reached extreme levels, with a decline in the incidence of violent conflict.

Higher degrees of inequality would, perhaps, be associated with extremes in the repressive capabilities of the state and elates. Nagel's version of the curvilinear relationship mapped differences in the intensity of violent conflict across societies marked along a range of degrees of inequality. However, it might be necessary to break down the relationship within particular societies. Thus, within a given society there might be both a sharp total range of inequality and also a series of smaller, more localised gaps in wealth, income, opportunity and so on.

Potentially, these smaller but more localised gaps might be more relevant in the origin of violent conflicts than the full social spread captured, for example, in a single Gini coefficient. Formally, this might represent a curvilinear relationship between inequality and violence where inequality is increasing in localised areas, while national distributional extremes are less relevant to conflict. In other words, a curvilinear relationship might hold at local levels irrespective of whether total social inequality is high or low by comparison with other societies.

Alternatively, local distributional conflicts over a relatively short range of inequality may combine with the dynamics of conflict related to grander national inequality (or, indeed, to other causes). André and Platteau, for example, argue that inequality nationally was not the prime source of the paroxysm of violence in Rwanda in 1994, but that, nonetheless, the increasing local level intensity of distributional tension contributed to the speed with which political violence spread through Rwandan society. Their own evidence shows an increasing intensity of local social conflict and disputes as a consequence of demographic pressure plus extensive rather than intensive agricultural development policies. The productivity constraint arising from this policy led to a shrinkage of average farm sizes and the emergence of a (formally illegal) land market, thanks to distress sales. Thus, some people were able to accumulate larger land holdings, generating inequality and tension. Other evidence suggests that while the overall Gini coefficient for Rwanda may not be extremely high by international standards, it is both an underestimate and on the increase.

A related example is Kriger's work on peasant involvement in the liberation war in Zimbabwe. According to this argument, the liberation war did not succeed on the basis of the mobilisation of the rural masses around a national redistribution project but because of the combination of nationalist ideologies with a patchwork of localised agendas of change, most involving one or another form of control over allocation decisions—for example, young men's interest in overturning gerontocratic village order, or women's struggles with men.

Within studies of the linkages of inequality to conflict, there is a distinction between arguments favouring the central role of land inequality and those stressing the significance of national and principally urban income inequality. André and Platteau's argument takes an intermediate and subtle position in this debate: claiming that rising land and economic inequality in rural Rwanda (driven by population increase and agricultural policies that failed to encourage intensification) was a secondary causal factor in the genocide, helping to determine the intensity of violence but not its basic origin. Others are more direct in their claims.

For example, Bains-marie et al. reduce a range of very different examples of principally rural violent conflict into a set of outcomes produced by unequal land distribution. Cases as divergent as El Salvador and post-independence Mozambique come to support the claim that as well as static and dynamic efficiency costs, large farms and the land inequality that goes with them entail social costs including unrest and civil war.Russett presented evidence of a linear relationship between the land tenure Gini coefficient and a cumulated score of violent political deaths (per million population) from 1950–1962, for 47 countries. And Huntington's argued that "Where the conditions of landownership... are inequitable and where the peasant lives in poverty and suffering, revolution is likely, if not inevitable, unless the government takes prompt measures to remedy these conditions".

Midlarsky and Roberts argue that El Salvador and Nicaragua bear out the "land mal-distribution" hypothesis, since compared to other middle-income developing countries, they experienced above average population growth in the 1950s and 1960s, their land Gini scores (around 0.8) were well above the global mean of 0.6, and landless households represented a high proportion of the total labour force. Muller and Seligson, however, argue that this case is weakened by a closer comparison within the Central American region. Both Costa Rica and Panama, during the same period, were characterised by remarkably similar preconditions (presumed often to be the "objective conditions of grievance and conflict") and yet remained peaceful. Costa Rica's population growth rate from 1960 to 1970 was, at 3.4 per cent annually, higher than Nicaragua's or El Salvador's and among the highest in the world. Land concentration as captured in the land Gini coefficient was about the same in Costa Rica and Panama as it was in El Salvador and Nicaragua; and the first two countries also had substantial shares of landless households in the total labour force.

Against these arguments—proposing linear or curvilinear relationships between inequality and violent political conflict or contrasting land with national income inequality, and from a variety of analytical perspectives—there are other claims that inequality simply is not a significant causal variable in the origins of conflict. Collier states: "Inequality does not seem to affect the risk of conflict. Rebellion does not seem to be the rage of the poor. ... Conflict is not caused by divisions, rather it actively needs to create them." Using the same Deininger and Squire dataset mined by Nafziger and Auvinen with some of their own interpolations, Fearon and Laitin find contrary results: notably, that, whether in a bivariate model or part of a multivariate equation, the Gini coefficient estimates "do not come close to either statistical or substantive significance.

The poor quality of the inequality data, available for only 108 countries, does not allow us to go beyond the claim that there appears to be no powerful cross-national relationship between inequality and civil war onset". Mitchell and Parvin also offered evidence that, if anything, equality was more disturbing of social peace than higher inequality, which—through a combination of encouraging expectations of mobility and an increase in the repressive powers of elates—would contain conflict.

An early version of Collier's models of civil war also set out the hypothesis that higher degrees of inequality would be a disincentive to rebellion, since under these conditions it would be expected that elates would allow the state to raise taxation on their wealth in order to fund a military response sufficient to protect the status quo. Weed, among others, gives evidence in support of this argument that basically there is no meaningful relationship, and thus that violent political conflict is typically caused by factors other than inequality. A final point here is to note that, historically, inequality varies very little and very slowly, and yet violent conflict and political violence appear to fluctuate more widely. Hence, at the very least, inequality must be insufficient to explain conflict, whether or not it is necessary.

Such an array of hypotheses and claims is bewildering. One explanation might be, as Lichbach argues, that the authors of different studies do not read one another; and that there is a babble of monologues rather than any constructive dialogue. "For example, students of black protest in the United States and of conflict cross-nationally have both been concerned with the EI-PC nexus, yet both have neglected each other's work". There have been some efforts to overcome this; for example, the World Bank's Web guide to inequality and its linkages to economic performance and social phenomena includes literature on violent crime as well as on civil war.

Nonetheless, to some extent there is still a problem of insufficient engagement across studies and, indeed, methodologies. However, this can only help explain part of the problem. As we have seen, even studies using the same dataset (for example, Deininger and Squire's inequality dataset) come to different conclusions about the relationship between income inequality and violent political conflict, civil war or complex humanitarian emergencies. This suggests that estimations of the relationship in statistical studies are sensitive to model specification and/or sampling variations. However, there are two larger issues that probably help to account for the cacophony of claims about inequality and its sociopolitical consequences.

Empirical Problems

Some of those who have recently argued that inequality is not a cause of political violence acknowledge that inequality data are highly imperfect and that this clouds our assessment of the relevance of inequality in conflict models. Thus Collier and Hoeffler note that "there is insufficient data to introduce distributional considerations into the empirical analysis". Meanwhile, as mentioned earlier, Fearon and Laitin state that because of the poor quality of the inequality data, it is difficult to go beyond the claim that there is no cross-national relationship between inequality and the onset of civil war. Therefore, rather than using this problem as a basis for rejecting the political significance of inequality in its entirety and substituting some other claim, the role of inequality might simply evade this kind of quantitative analysis.

This empirical problem is in fact extreme. It extends beyond the quality of Gini coefficient data, though it certainly encompasses this issue. There are great difficulties in the measurements of both dependent and independent variables in trying to assess the role of inequality in the origin of violent political conflict. Data on income inequality are often insufficient, especially as a basis of inter-country comparison. Measuring land inequality is far from straightforward. And there are problems with available data (as well as categorical bases of datasets) for violence and conflict.

Recent research into economic inequality in Latin America confirms the dangers of building causal arguments on inequality data. Székely and Hilgert), analysing household survey data from 18 Latin American countries, find that ranking among these countries in terms of conventional inequality indicators are illusory. Scores are driven by variations in the characteristics of the data and their treatment. Hence our "ideas about the effect of inequality on economic growth are also driven by quality and coverage differences in household surveys and by the way in which the data is [sic] treated".

This research only confirms the criticisms that have long been made of distributional data and the inferences that can be drawn from them. These criticisms arguably amount to more than modest qualifications: rather, they suggest that—even if it were methodologically supportable—it is not possible to draw credible inferences from the available data on inter-country comparison about patterns of event regularity involving inequality in wealth and income. The problem with inequality data is not exclusive to poor countries. Atkinson and Brandolini, for example, show the dramatic impact of adopting different datasets on inequality on rankings among countries of the Organisation for Economic Co-operation and Development (OECD).

If the focus is on "land inequality" rather than national income inequality (or the land Gini coefficient versus the national income Gini coefficient), there are still difficulties in measuring effectively for comparative purposes. For Central America up to the late 1970s, for example, the land Gini scores are virtually identical. Yet, historically, the structure of rural society in Central America has varied considerably. One may, for example, get more sense of variation from measures of "mini-fundisación", that is, of the extent of impoverished smallholders in the presence of large farms.

Thus Midlarsky's "patterned inequality" captures the concentration of land holdings between smallholders and large farm-holders across different countries; while Muller et al. propose an index of "bifurcated inequality" derived from the proportion of small farms and from the average sizes of small farms relative to large farms. Or one may focus on the share of total agricultural land dominated by the largest farms, to capture their control of land supply. Further, rural inequality involves tenancy, and tenancy arrangements vary widely in security and the income-generating potential of the land they farm. Beyond this it is necessary to examine also the characteristics of rural labour markets and how these mediate conditions of life and political organisation.

Meanwhile, there are considerable complications with the empirical analysis of "violent political conflict". These complications take two main forms: the reliability of evidence for instances and degrees of intensity of conflict; and the choice of categorisation systems. The first problems arise with the reporting of violence. In wartime, health information systems and, particularly, civil registration systems that would record deaths and their causes, often break down).

Moreover, there are complications of interest as well as practical constraints that undermine reliable data collection involving political violence, armed conflict or even some forms of interpersonal or "social" violence. Research from the Medical Research Council in South Africa, for example, uses the analytical device of an "iceberg of sexual violence and coercion": rapes reported to and recorded by the police represent only the tip protruding above the social surface. In northeast Africa, there have been claims of a trend of rising violent conflict between herders and farmers; however, it is difficult to confirm or reject such claims when there are only occasional and variable exercises in recording such conflict and, thus, there is no reliable time-series data.

As Murray et al. point out, most published analyses of deaths from conflict have relied on press reports of eyewitness accounts and of official pronouncements from conflict contestants. Both sources are clearly subject to error and political manipulation. Brockett argues that it is difficult to assess the relative merits of competing arguments concerning the political consequences of land inequality when they rely on "the grossly inaccurate data set provided by the World Handbook of Political and Social Indicators". It is not just that this dataset underestimates the incidence of political violence in various countries, but, more significantly, that "a more accurate reporting would alter both the rankings between countries and the magnitude of the intervals between country scores, thereby substantially altering quantitative analyses utilising this data set".

Thus, "the Handbook reports deaths in Honduras during the mid-1970s as twice as numerous as in either El Salvador or Guatemala! In reality, Honduras would rank fourth with Guatemala far ahead for all five". Remote rural deaths are less likely to attract news coverage than urban assassinations. Brockett also gives an example of variation in news coverage tied to particular interests. In 1975 a "bananagate" scandal involving a US multinational's allegedly corrupt ties to the president of Honduras led to unprecedented coverage of Honduran affairs in the New York Times, including a mention of six people killed at a peasant training centre in June of that year. Similar incidents prior to the scandal had gone unremarkable the next person one meets is from a different ethnic group in a given country—the "ethno-linguistic fragmentation index". However, measuring diversity is not entirely straightforward. One clear example is Schetter's observation that for Afghanistan one estimate puts the number of ethnic groups in the country at 200, while another study estimates 50 different groups.

A further problem is the counting of indirect and non-battlefield deaths. Kaldor, among others, claims that the ratio of civilian to military deaths in war had swung from 1:8 in the early twentieth century to roughly 8:1 by the end of the century. The ratio of indirect to direct conflict deaths has been quoted in recent years as 9:1. However, these claims have slightly shaky foundations that are not always acknowledged. Murray et al. cite one cross-sectional study indicating that "the total disability adjusted life years lost in 1999 due to the indirect effects of military conflicts occurring between 1991 and 1997 was about the same as the number lost due to the direct effects of all wars in 1999".

A different kind of empirical problem arises in establishing classification systems as the basis of datasets for statistical studies. At one level, this is a matter of selecting the coding rules to adopt: which rules determine whether a particular conflict, for example, is included in a dataset on "civil wars". At another level it is a matter of whether the civil war category itself, or any other, is a valid one. Zambians discusses in detail the problems of different rules applied to the inclusion or exclusion of events from civil war datasets—a variation that holds in some cases even for researchers claiming to use the same coding system. The main obstacles include the setting of a threshold for inclusion of a conflict as a "proper" civil war and deciding whether or not to include non-battlefield, civilian deaths. Variations in coding civil wars lead to substantial differences in the results of regressions of the most typical variables used in civil war models on the incidence of such conflicts. However, one can question why a specific dataset of civil wars makes sense. From the perspective of research on inequality and

Brazil is characterised by an extraordinary array of forms of social and political violence—from the "everyday violence" suffered by the poor (both actual physical violence and "structural violence"), through the violent conflicts surrounding the institutionalisation of private property rights on the northern Amazonian frontier and the conflict between large landowners (in some cases with police connivance) and the landless movement, the Movement Sem Terras (MST), to the urban violence of "funk balls", drug-related violence, against street children, and the institutionalised incentives encouraging police violence). The distribution of income and wealth in Brazil is widely accepted to be one of the most unequal in the world. For example, Deininger and Squire give a Gini observation (with an "OK" quality assurance) of 63.42 for 1989. Sutc life shows, in one illustration of Brazilian inequality, that average wages of Brazilian white males are some three times greater than those of their black male compatriots.

Studies of the relationship between economic inequality and violent political conflict have looked at a range of categories of violence and conflict, from homicide rates to civil wars. Sometimes claims are made that shorten the results of different studies without fully acknowledging these differences. For example, Nafziger and Auvinen draw on the claims of Alesina and Perotti for their argument that inequality does matter in the origins of CHEs. Yet Alesina and Perotti claimed to find a pattern linking inequality with political instability measured through the incidence of political assassinations, which is a very different category from the CHEs.

There is possibly a need for more direct research on the whole range of manifestations of social violence and violent political (collective) conflict. Alternatively, there is a need to focus on a greater range of more specifically defined categories. For the analytical challenge is to establish constructive categorisation systems that help to reveal more than they obscure, given that virtually all classification systems impose artificial discontinuities on reality. The problems are especially intense where variation within a given category is as great as that between categories. This is almost certainly the case, for example, with the distinction between "civil wars" and other political conflicts.

The upshot is that there are no grounds for accepting any "event regularity" holding across countries when it comes to inequality and its consequences for violent conflict. There is a baffling array of empirical claims. The data on which statistical studies of the problem are based are massively unreliable. And the literature has paid too little attention to the pitfalls of commonly used classification systems and their implications for the enquiry into the consequences of inequality. Faced with this predicament, some take the view that one can quietly discard the problem and push an alternative claim about the causes of violent political conflict. However, the real implication of such uncertainty is the nagging possibility that inequality might still be significant, at least sometimes and to the origins or "epidemiology" of some conflicts.

Processes, Mechanisms and Relations

All the statistical studies reviewed above are focused on outcomes. They relate the observable, specifically quantifiable (arguably, at any rate), facts and signs of inequality. They are propelled by a widespread belief in the possibility of finding event regularities of a probabilities kind, captured by econometric, polimetrics and in historical studies by climacteric analysis. At least for the study of inequality-conflict linkages, they have not been very successful. This should encourage an exploration into what lies behind this quantifiable surface, and into the causes of the inequality that various techniques try to measure.

Since it is not likely to be just the fact of inequality or even a given degree of measurable intensity of inequality that provokes a certain class of political or social outcomes such as civil war, it is worth looking deeper into the processes, mechanisms and relations that generate and sustain inequality. Hirschman's notion of the varying "tolerance for inequality" is one route to this enquiry. More recently, Stewart's analysis of "horizontal inequality" is another. And Tilly's concept of "categorical inequality" sustained by particular mechanisms is, arguably, the most fruitful recent contribution.

Hirschman's reflections of the proposed workings of a "tunnel effect" were prompted specifically by two episodes of violent political conflict in the late 1960s and early 1970s: the Biafra war in Nigeria and the civil war in Pakistan leading to the independence of Bangladesh. Observing that both these "development disasters" followed periods of developmental surges rather than the protracted stagnation so commonly associated nowadays with civil wars, Hirschman argued for the existence of a social mechanism that could suppress relative deprivation, the frustration-aggression nexus, or, more plainly, envy. As development proceeded, some people's fortunes improved while others were left behind, and thus inequality typically increased.

But the expectations of those left behind might be raised rather than overwhelmed by bitterness. Greater inequality effectively gave information about social and economic change that could be interpreted as a signal of hope even for those not immediately benefiting from development. However, this tunnel effect must be qualified. First, it would not last indefinitely and would at some stage stop functioning. Second, the suspension of envy would be unlikely to operate where the opportunities provided by economic development were, or were seen to be, monopolised by certain groups, while excluding others. Third, beneficiaries of change are not always politically quiet or supportive of inequality: a plausible overlapping of the end of the tunnel effect with the continued politicisation of educated middle-class urbanites around redistributed objectives would provide the classic conditions of revolutionary coalition building.

There are elements in Hirschman's analysis of the changing tolerance for inequality of an interest in what has come to be known recently as "horizontal inequality". Thus, Stewart argues that most studies of the relationship between economic inequality and political conflict have understood it only in terms of "vertical inequality", that is, the distribution of income across the whole population of individuals from richest to poorest and as captured by the Gini coefficient. However, she argues, horizontal inequality is far more significant, reflecting as it does differential standards of living and access to public sector employment, political rights, education opportunities, and so on among collective groups within a society.

These groups might fall into various classification kinds, for example, religious, regional, class or ethnic. On this basis, Stewart constructs a matrix of possibilities, while acknowledging the difficulty in pinning down precisely (by quantitative scores, for example) the comparative role of horizontal inequality across a sample of countries. On one hand, this scheme of horizontal inequality is simply another form of outcome description, a 90-degree rotation of vertical inequality, as it were.

On the other hand, however, the conception in terms of exclusion from certain rights and opportunities, as well as a focus on average income levels, shifts attention to discriminatory social relationships. Stewart's matrix of horizontal inequality raises many questions and qualifications, some of which she herself addresses. For example, why is it that a situation of high intragroup inequality in Kenya (among the Kikuyu) seemed to work against collection action to redress exclusion from the chief political opportunities, while high intragroup inequality in Rwanda (among the Hutus) did not stop mass murder through a deflective, scapegoating mechanism?

The politics of inequality and the significance of varying degrees of institutionalisation of group inequality are issues tackled in Tilly's framework of "categorical inequality". Like Hirschman, Tilly effectively discusses the tolerance for inequality, addressing the question of the extraordinary durability of social inequality and highlighting the mechanisms that account for this durability.

However, perhaps in a similar vein to the horizontal inequality analysis and dovetailing to some extent with Hirschman's note on heterogeneous societies, Tilly's framework highlights inequality between social pairings—citizens versus non-citizens, men and women, black and white, Anglican and Catholic in pre-emancipation England, the differential property rights of large landowners and peasants, and so on. Categorical inequality is distinguished sharply from the continuous distributions of income captured by, say, the Gini coefficient and in some cases tying inequality in income to returns to the purported distributions of individual attributes.

In this organisational (rather than principally individual or ideological) analysis, inequality between categorical pairings is sustained by social mechanisms: exploitation is at its core; where there is exploitation there is, typically, opportunity hoarding by one group (of access to jobs, control of certain markets, political position and so on); emulation spreads categorical inequality through various branches of a society and internationally; and adaptation ensures that even the disadvantaged develop footholds of survival and acquiescence in the system.

In this approach, exclusion is not simply a negative, an absence, but a directly relational factor that is at the same time a form of inclusion in a given social system. Where the state takes a direct interest in creating and supporting categorical inequality, as is common, it adds the coercive element that further fixes the paired inequality. According to this perspective, redressing this kind of inequality is only possible through sustained political action and in circumstances where the benefits accruing to the beneficiaries from exploitation and/or opportunity hoarding fade and the costs of maintaining the system rise.

Examples would include the rising cost of discrimination against English Roman Catholics during international wars, when legal restrictions prevented the army from recruiting Irish Catholic soldiers; and the rising cost to South African capitalists of that most extreme form of institutionalised categorical inequality, apartheid. For the most part, the "histories of landlord-tenant relations, religious inequalities, and social movements indicate... that organisers generally have a difficult time stimulating shared awareness of oppression and determination to resist, that even with intense organising efforts they fail except in special structural circumstances".

It is true that there is little to distinguish, in Tilly's analysis, between various types of inequality. Some might argue, as does Wood, that the difference that constitutes class identity "is, by definition, a relationship of inequality and power, in a way that sexual or cultural 'difference' need not be". This might lead one to look for varied types of political conflict over inequality—where, for example, the intensity of conflict might be greater where the fundamental form of exploitation and the character of direct relationships of power and inequality defining society are at stake. In such conditions—essentially those of that protracted, disruptive, uneven moment of transition commonly known as development—it is also worth noting the relations among relations, or the relations between identity sources.

Thus, the fundamental institutional arrangements of power and exploitation may be in flux and at stake, and may be seen in class terms (such as landlords, peasants, wage labourers and capitalists), but political mobilisation in reaction to the social crisis often takes other identity terms. Hobsbawm for example, stresses how ethnic nationalism is typically a defensive reaction to modern, transitional crises. This fundamental developmental perspective is not always stressed even in the process-related or relational accounts of inequality and conflict, or indeed the outcome-based statistical explorations of the problem. And yet the fundamental upheaval of capitalist development must be central to most modern violent political conflict.

Capitalist development, or industrialisation, is the modern form of a more general phenomenon of transition—or socialite metamorphosis. In transition, as Gellner argued "tomorrow is not just another day; it is an other day, altogether". From this perspective, illiberal politics and violent conflict are unsurprising features of what might be called—re-inventing Gramsci's use of the phrase—a "war of position". Retreating from class analysis, even formal economic theorists have engaged with this predicament. Pagano, for example, draws on Fred Hirsch's concept of "position goods" to argue that the fact that consumption by some people of certain "goods" necessarily implies their "negative consumption" by others and that, consequently, the existence of such goods makes conflict likely.

4

Alcoholism

Alcoholism, also known as alcohol dependence, is a disabling addictive disorder. It is characterized by compulsive and uncontrolled consumption of alcohol despite its negative effects on the drinker's health, relationships, and social standing. Like other drug addictions, alcoholism is medically defined as a treatable disease. The term "alcoholism" is a widely used term first coined in 1849 by Magnus Huss, but in medicine the term was replaced by "alcohol abuse" and "alcohol dependence" in the 1980s DSM III. Similarly in 1979 an expert World Health Organisation committee disfavoured the use of "alcoholism" as a diagnostic entity, preferring the category of "alcohol dependence syndrome". In the 19th and early 20th centuries, alcohol dependence was called dipsomania before the term "alcoholism" replaced it.

The biological mechanisms underpinning alcoholism are uncertain, however, risk factors include social environment, stress, mental health, genetic predisposition, age, ethnic group, and sex. Long-term alcohol abuse produces physiological changes in the brain such as tolerance and physical dependence. Such brain chemistry changes maintain the alcoholic's compulsive inability to stop drinking and result in alcohol withdrawal syndrome upon discontinuation of alcohol consumption. Alcohol damages almost every organ in the body, including the brain; because of the cumulative toxic effects of chronic alcohol abuse, the alcoholic risks suffering a range of medical and psychiatric disorders. Alcoholism has profound social consequences for alcoholics and the people of their lives.

Alcoholism is the cyclic presence of tolerance, withdrawal, and excessive alcohol use; the drinker's inability to control such compulsive drinking, despite awareness of its harm to his or her health, indicate that the person might be an alcoholic.

Questionnaire-based screening is a method of detecting harmful drinking patterns, including alcoholism. Alcohol detoxification is conducted to withdraw the alcoholic person from drinking alcohol, usually with cross-tolerance drugs, e.g. benzodiazepines to manage withdrawal symptoms. Post-medical care, such as group therapy, or self-help groups, usually is required to maintain alcoholic abstention.

Often, alcoholics also are addicted to other drugs, most often benzodiazepines, which might require additional medical treatment. The alcoholic woman is more sensitive to alcohol's deleterious physical, cerebral, and mental effects, and increased social stigma, in relation to a man, for being an alcoholic. The World Health Organisation estimates that there are 140 million alcoholics worldwide.

Alcohol Misuse

Alcoholism is characterised by an increased tolerance of and physical dependence on alcohol, affecting an individual's ability to control alcohol consumption safely. These characteristics are believed to play a role in impeding an alcoholic's ability to stop drinking. Alcoholism can have adverse effects on mental health, causing psychiatric disorders to develop and an increased risk of suicide.

Physical Symptoms

Long term alcohol abuse can cause a number of physical symptoms, including cirrhosis of the liver, pancreatitis, epilepsy, polyneuropathy, alcoholic dementia, heart disease, nutritional deficiencies, and sexual dysfunction, and can eventually be fatal. Other physical effects include an increased risk of developing cardiovascular disease, malabsorption, alcoholic liver disease, and cancer. Damage to the central nervous system and peripheral nervous system can occur from sustained alcohol consumption.

Women develop long-term complications of alcohol dependence more rapidly than do men. Additionally, women have a higher mortality rate from alcoholism than men. Examples of long term complications include brain, heart, and liver damage and an increased risk of breast cancer. Additionally, heavy drinking over time has been found to have a negative effect on reproductive functioning in women. This results in reproductive dysfunction such as anovulation, decreased ovarian mass, problems or irregularity of the menstrual cycle, and early menopause. Alcoholic ketoacidosis can occur in individuals who chronically abuse alcohol and have a recent history of binge drinking.

Psychiatric Symptoms

Long term misuse of alcohol can cause a wide range of mental health problems. Severe cognitive problems are not uncommon; approximately 10 percent of all dementia cases are related to alcohol consumption, making it the second leading cause of dementia. Excessive alcohol use causes damage to brain function, and psychological health can be increasingly affected over time.

Psychiatric disorders are common in alcoholics, with as many as 25 percent suffering severe psychiatric disturbances.

The most prevalent psychiatric symptoms are anxiety and depression disorders. Psychiatric symptoms usually initially worsen during alcohol withdrawal, but typically improve or disappear with continued abstinence. Psychosis, confusion, and organic brain syndrome may be caused by alcohol misuse, which can lead to a misdiagnosis such as schizophrenia. Panic disorder can develop or worsen as a direct result of long term alcohol misuse.

The co-occurrence of major depressive disorder and alcoholism is well documented. Among those with comorbid occurrences, a distinction is commonly made between depressive episodes that remit with alcohol abstinence ("substance-induced"), and depressive episodes that are primary and do not remit with abstinence ("independent" episodes). Additional use of other drugs may increase the risk of depression.

Psychiatric disorders differ depending on gender. Women who have alcohol-use disorders often have a co-occurring psychiatric diagnosis such as major depression, anxiety, panic disorder, bulimia, post-traumatic stress disorder (PTSD), or borderline personality disorder. Men with alcohol-use disorders more often have a co-occurring diagnosis of narcissistic or antisocial personality disorder, bipolar disorder, schizophrenia, impulse disorders or attention deficit/hyperactivity disorder. Women with alcoholism are more likely to have a history of physical or sexual assault, abuse and domestic violence than those in the general population, which can lead to higher instances of psychiatric disorders and greater dependence on alcohol.

Social Effects

The social problems arising from alcoholism are serious, caused by the pathological changes in the brain and the intoxicating effects of alcohol. Alcohol abuse is associated with an increased risk of committing criminal offences, including child abuse, domestic violence, rape, burglary and assault. Alcoholism is associated with loss of employment, which can lead to financial problems. Drinking at inappropriate times, and behavior caused by reduced judgment, can lead to legal consequences, such as criminal charges for drunk driving or public disorder, or civil penalties for tortious behavior, and may lead to a criminal sentence.

An alcoholic's behavior and mental impairment, while drunk, can profoundly impact those surrounding them and lead to isolation from family and friends. This isolation can lead to marital conflict and divorce, or contribute to domestic violence. Alcoholism can also lead to child neglect, with subsequent lasting damage to the emotional development of the alcoholic's children.

Alcohol Withdrawal

As with similar substances with a sedative-hypnotic mechanism, such as barbiturates and benzodiazepines, withdrawal from alcohol dependence can be fatal if it is not properly managed. Alcohol's primary effect is the increase in stimulation of the GABAA receptor, promoting central nervous system depression. With repeated heavy consumption of alcohol, these receptors are desensitized and reduced in number, resulting in tolerance and physical dependence. When alcohol consumption is stopped too abruptly, the person's nervous system suffers from uncontrolled synapse firing. This can result in symptoms that include anxiety, life threatening seizures, delirium tremens, hallucinations, shakes and possible heart failure. Other neurotransmitter systems are also involved, especially dopamine and NMDA.

Acute withdrawal symptoms tend to subside after one to three weeks. Less severe symptoms (e.g. insomnia and anxiety, anhedonia) may continue as part of a post withdrawal syndrome gradually improving with abstinence for a year or more. Withdrawal symptoms begin to subside as the body and central nervous system restore alcohol tolerance and GABA functioning towards normal.

Causes of Alcoholism

A complex mixture of genetic and environmental factors influence the risk of the development of alcoholism. Genes which influence the metabolism of alcohol also influence the risk of alcoholism, and may be indicated by a family history of alcoholism. One paper has found that alcohol use at an early age may influence the expression of genes which increase the risk of alcohol dependence. Individuals who have a genetic disposition to alcoholism are also more likely to begin drinking at an earlier age than average. Also, a younger age of onset of drinking is associated with an increased risk of the development of alcoholism, and about 40 percent of alcoholics will drink excessively by their late adolescence. It is not entirely clear whether this association is causal, and some researchers have been known to disagree with this view.

Severe childhood trauma is also associated with an general increase in the risk of drug dependency. Lack of peer and family support is associated with a increased risk of alcoholism developing. Genetics and adolescence are associated with an increased sensitivity to the neurotoxic effects of chronic alcohol abuse. Cortical degeneration due to the neurotoxic effects increases impulsive behaviour, which may contribute to the development, persistence and severity of alcohol use disorders. There is evidence that with abstinence, there is a reversal of at least some of the alcohol induced central nervous system damage.

Alcohol's primary effect is the increase in stimulation of the GABAA receptor, promoting central nervous system depression. With repeated heavy consumption of alcohol, these receptors are desensitized and reduced in number, resulting in tolerance and physical dependence. The amount of alcohol that can be biologically processed and its effects differ between sexes. Equal dosages of alcohol consumed by men and women generally result in women having higher blood alcohol concentrations (BACs). This can be attributed to many reasons, the main being that women have less body water than men. A given amount of alcohol, therefore becomes more highly concentrated in a woman's body. A given amount of alcohol causes greater intoxication for women due to different hormone release compared to men.

Prevention of Alcoholism

The World Health Organization, the European Union and other regional bodies, national governments and parliaments have formed alcohol policies in order to reduce the harm of alcoholism. Targeting adolescents and young adults is regarded as an important step to reduce the harm of alcohol abuse. Increasing the age at which licit drugs of abuse such as alcohol can be purchased, the banning or restricting advertising of alcohol has been recommended as additional ways of reducing the harm of alcohol dependence and abuse. Credible, evidence based educational campaigns in the mass media about the consequences of alcohol abuse have been recommended. Guidelines for parents to prevent alcohol abuse amongst adolescents, and for helping young people with mental health problems have also been suggested.

Management

Treatments are varied because there are multiple perspectives of alcoholism. Those who approach alcoholism as a medical condition or disease recommend differing treatments than, for instance, those who approach the condition as one of social choice. Most treatments focus on helping people discontinue their alcohol intake, followed up with life training and/or social support in order to help them resist a return to alcohol use. Since alcoholism involves multiple factors which encourage a person to continue drinking, they must all be addressed in order to successfully prevent a relapse. An example of this kind of treatment is detoxification followed by a combination of supportive therapy, attendance at self-help groups, and ongoing development of coping mechanisms. The treatment community for alcoholism typically supports an abstinence-based zero tolerance approach; however, there are some who promote a harm-reduction approach as well.

Detoxification

Alcohol detoxification or 'detox' for alcoholics is an abrupt stop of alcohol drinking coupled with the substitution of drugs, such as benzodiazepines, that have similar effects to prevent alcohol withdrawal. Individuals who are only at risk of mild to moderate withdrawal symptoms can be detoxified as outpatients. Individuals at risk of a severe withdrawal syndrome as well as those who have significant or acute comorbid conditions are generally treated as inpatients. Detoxification does not actually treat alcoholism, and it is necessary to follow-up detoxification with an appropriate treatment program for alcohol dependence or abuse in order to reduce the risk of relapse.

Group Therapy

Various forms of group therapy or psychotherapy can be used to deal with underlying psychological issues that are related to alcohol addiction, as well as provide relapse prevention skills. The mutual-help group-counseling approach is one of the most common ways of helping alcoholics maintain sobriety. Alcoholics Anonymous was one of the first organizations formed to provide mutual, nonprofessional counseling, and it is still the largest. Others include LifeRing Secular Recovery, SMART Recovery, and Women For Sobriety.

Rationing and Moderation

Rationing and moderation programs such as Moderation Management and DrinkWise do not mandate complete abstinence. While most alcoholics are unable to limit their drinking in this way, some return to moderate drinking. A 2002 U.S. study by the National Institute on Alcohol Abuse and Alcoholism (NIAAA) showed that 17.7 percent of individuals diagnosed as alcohol dependent more than one year prior returned to low-risk drinking. This group, however, showed fewer initial symptoms of dependency. A follow-up study, using the same subjects that were judged to be in remission in 2001–2002, examined the rates of return to problem drinking in 2004–2005. The study found abstinence from alcohol was the most stable form of remission for recovering alcoholics. A long-term (60 year) follow-up of two groups of alcoholic men concluded that "return to controlled drinking rarely persisted for much more than a decade without relapse or evolution into abstinence."

Medications

A variety of medications may be prescribed as part of treatment for alcoholism. Some of the medications currently in use are:

— *Antabuse* (disulfiram) prevents the elimination of acetaldehyde, a chemical the body produces when breaking down ethanol. Acetaldehyde itself is the cause of many hangover symptoms from alcohol use. The overall effect is severe discomfort when alcohol is ingested: an extremely fast-acting and long-lasting uncomfortable hangover. This discourages an alcoholic from drinking in significant amounts while they take the medicine. A recent 9-year study found that incorporation of supervised disulfiram and the related compound carbamide into a comprehensive treatment program resulted in an abstinence rate of over 50 percent.

— *Temposil* (calcium carbimide) works in the same way as Antabuse; it has an advantage in that the occasional adverse effects of disulfiram, hepatotoxicity and drowsiness, do not occur with calcium carbimide.

— *Naltrexone* is a competitive antagonist for opioid receptors, effectively blocking the effects of endorphins and opiates. Naltrexone is used to decrease cravings for alcohol and encourage abstinence. Alcohol causes the body to release endorphins, which in turn release dopamine and activate the reward pathways; hence when naltrexone is in the body there is a reduction in the pleasurable effects from consuming alcohol. Naltrexone is also used in an alcoholism treatment method called the Sinclair Method, which treats patients through a combination of Naltrexone and continued drinking.

— *Campral* (acamprosate) stabilises the brain chemistry that is altered due to alcohol dependence via antagonising the actions of glutamate, a neurotransmitter which is hyperactive in the post-withdrawal phase.

Epidemiology

Substance use disorders are a major public health problem facing many countries. "The most common substance of abuse/dependence in patients presenting for treatment is alcohol." In the United Kingdom, the number of 'dependent drinkers' was calculated as over 2.8 million in 2001. About 12% of American adults have had an alcohol dependence problem at some time in their life. The World Health

Organization estimates that about 140 million people throughout the world suffer from alcohol dependence. In the United States and western Europe 10 to 20 percent of men and 5 to 10 percent of women at some point in their lives will meet criteria for alcoholism.

Within the medical and scientific communities, there is broad consensus regarding alcoholism as a disease state. For example, the American Medical Association considers alcohol a drug and states that "drug addiction is a chronic, relapsing brain disease characterized by compulsive drug seeking and use despite often devastating consequences. It results from a complex interplay of biological vulnerability, environmental exposure, and developmental factors (e.g., stage of brain maturity)."

Alcoholism has a higher prevalence among men, though in recent decades, the proportion of female alcoholics has increased. Current evidence indicates that in both men and women, alcoholism is 50–60 percent genetically determined, leaving 40–50 percent for environmental influences. Most alcoholics develop alcoholism during adolescence or young adulthood.

A 2002 study by the National Institute on Alcohol Abuse and Alcoholism surveyed a group of 1,122 adults meeting the criteria for alcohol dependence and found that after one year, some met the authors' criteria for low-risk drinking, even though only 25.5 percent of the group received any treatment, with the breakdown as follows: 25 percent were found to be still dependent, 27.3 percent were in partial remission (some symptoms persist), 11.8 percent asymptomatic drinkers (consumption increases chances of relapse) and 35.9 percent were fully recovered — made up of 17.7 percent low-risk drinkers plus 18.2 percent abstainers.

In contrast, however, the results of a long term (60 year) follow-up of two groups of alcoholic men by George

Vaillant at Harvard Medical School indicated that "return to controlled drinking rarely persisted for much more than a decade without relapse or evolution into abstinence." Vaillant also noted that "return-to-controlled drinking, as reported in short-term studies, is often a mirage."

The most common cause of death in alcoholics is from cardiovascular complications. There is a high rate of suicide in chronic alcoholics, which increases the longer a person drinks. This is believed to be due to alcohol causing physiological distortion of brain chemistry, as well as social isolation. Suicide is also very common in adolescent alcohol abusers, with 25 percent of suicides in adolescents being related to alcohol abuse. Approximately 18 percent of alcoholics commit suicide, and research has found that over 50 percent of all suicides are associated with alcohol or drug dependence. The figure is higher for adolescents, with alcohol or drug misuse playing a role in up to 70 percent of suicides.

Alcohol has a long history of use and misuse throughout recorded human history. Biblical, Egyptian and Babylonian sources record history of abuse and dependence on alcohol. In some ancient cultures alcohol was worshiped and others its abuse was condemned. Excessive alcohol misuse and drunkenness were recognised as causing problems thousand of years ago. However, the defining of habitual drunkenness as it was then known as and its adverse consequences were not well established medically until the 18th century. In 1647 a Greek monk was the first to document that chronic alcohol misuse was associated with toxicity to the nervous system and body which resulted in a range of medical disorders such as seizures, paralysis and internal bleeding. In 1920 the effects of alcohol abuse and chronic drunkenness led to the failed prohibition of alcohol being considered and eventually enforced briefly in America. In 2005 the cost of alcohol dependence and abuse was estimated to cost the USA economy approximately 220 billion dollars per year, more than cancer and obesity.

Social and Cultural Problems

The various health problems associated with long-term alcohol consumption are generally perceived as detrimental to society, for example, money due to lost labor-hours, medical costs, and secondary treatment costs. Alcohol use is a major contributing factor for head injuries, motor vehicle accidents, violence, and assaults. Beyond money, there are also significant social costs to both the alcoholic and their family and friends. For instance, alcohol consumption by a pregnant woman can lead to fetal alcohol syndrome, an incurable and damaging condition.

Estimates of the economic costs of alcohol abuse, collected by the World Health Organization, vary from one to six percent of a country's GDP. One Australian estimate pegged alcohol's social costs at 24 percent of all drug abuse costs; a similar Canadian study concluded alcohol's share was 41 percent. One study quantified the cost to the UK of *all* forms of alcohol misuse in 2001 as £18.5–20 billion.

Stereotypes of alcoholics are often found in fiction and popular culture. The 'town drunk' is a stock character in Western popular culture. Stereotypes of drunkenness may be based on racism or xenophobia, as in the depiction of the Irish as heavy drinkers. Studies by social psychologists Stivers and Greeley attempt to document the perceived prevalence of high alcohol consumption amongst the Irish in America.

Alcoholism in Family Systems

Alcoholism in family systems refers to the conditions in families that enable alcoholism, and the effects of alcoholic behavior by one or more family members on the rest of the family. Mental health professionals are increasingly considering alcoholism and addiction as diseases that flourish in and are enabled by family systems. Family members react to the alcoholic with particular behavioral patterns. They may enable the addiction to continue by shielding the addict from the negative consequences of his actions. Such behaviors are referred to as codependence. In this way, the alcoholic is said to suffer from the disease of addiction, whereas the family members suffer from the disease of codependence.

Alcoholism is one of the leading causes of a dysfunctional family. As of 2001, there were an estimated 26.8 million children of alcoholics (COAs) in the United States, with as many as 11 million of them under than age of 18. Children of addicts have an increased suicide rate and on average have total health care costs 32 percent greater than children of nonalcoholic families.

Adults from alcoholic families experience higher levels of state and trait anxiety and lower levels of differentiation of self than adults raised in non-alcoholic families. Additionally adult children of alcoholics have lower self-esteem, excessive feelings of responsibility, difficulties reaching out, higher incidence of depression, and increased likelihood of becoming alcoholics.

Alcoholism does not have uniform effects on all families. The levels of dysfunction and resiliency of the non-alcoholic adults are important factors in effects on children in the family. Children of untreated alcoholics score lower on measures of family cohesion, intellectual-cultural orientation, active-recreational orientation, and independence. They have higher levels of conflict within the family, and many experience other family members as distant and non-communicative. The cumulative effect of the family dysfunction may affect the children in families with untreated alcoholics' ability to grow in developmentally healthy ways.

5

Drug Abuse

Since the 1960s, and in a context of rapid and deep socioeconomic changes throughout the world, the international drug control system has succeeded in containing the spread of annual illicit drug use to around 200 million people, or 5% of the world population aged 15-64. This compares very favourably with the much higher prevalence of tobacco use, which causes 5.4 million deaths per year. The system was set up to restrict the use of controlled drugs to medical and scientific purposes and, while containment of illicit use to relatively low levels is already a remarkable achievement, Member States have always had a more ambitious goal in mind.

In 1998, 37 years after the 1961 Single Convention, a special session of the UN General Assembly (UNGASS) decided to work towards the "elimination or significant reduction" of illicit drug production and abuse by 2008, and adopted a series of sectorial plans to reach that objective.

Gathered at the end of the 10-year period, Member States were not satisfied with the results and declared that they were still "gravely concerned about the growing threat posed by the world drug problem." There is no single measure of the year-on-year evolution of the world drug problem. There is not even a clear definition of what is meant by the expression the 'world drug problem'. Since public health is at the heart of the international drug control system, the prevalence of illicit drug use is generally considered a central, though imperfect, indicator of the status of the problem. Illicit drug use is a multifaceted issue, however.

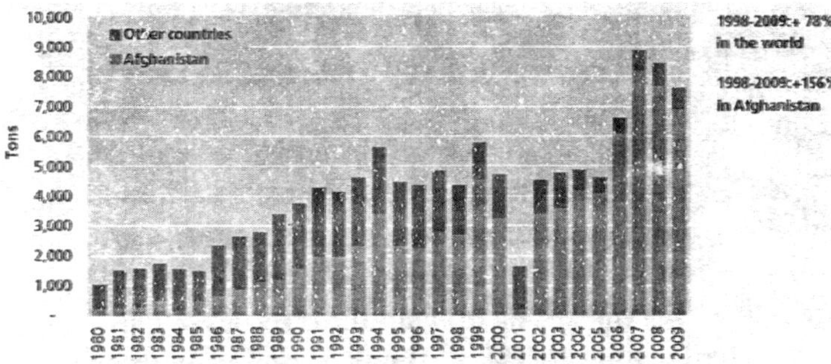

Figure 1. Global potential opium production, 1980-2009

In particular, different drugs produce different effects and present different risks to users. At the international level, annual prevalence of drug use, by drug category, has thus become the most standardised indicator to monitor the evolution of illicit drug use. Unfortunately, only a minority of countries have adequate national prevalence monitoring systems in place. Producing a precise, reliable and sensitive measure of the evolution of the world drug problem over the last decade on that basis is therefore very difficult.

Data on illicit drug supply can help fill the information gap, at least for some drugs. The bulk of cocaine and opium production is concentrated in a few locations and successful efforts to develop annual surveys in the context of the 1998 Plan of Action have provided a coverage that is systematic enough to closely follow the evolution of the global opiate and cocaine markets from the supply side.

Data on illicit opiates supply, arguably the most problematic drug category and always a core preoccupation of the international drug control regime, show that global opium production increased by close to 80% between 1998 and 2009. Increases in Afghanistan more than offset remarkable declines in South-East Asia during that period. There were encouraging declines in the last three years, but Afghan production was still more than 150% higher in 2009 than in 1998. With strong increases after 2005, production seems to have well exceeded world demand and led to the creation of large stockpiles, but it is clear that the global opiate market has not been eliminated, or significantly reduced, since 1998.

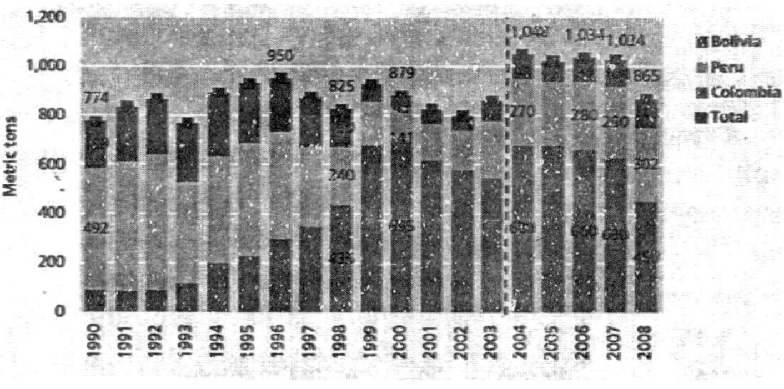

Figure 2. Global potential cocaine production (Mt.), 1990-2008

The evolution of cocaine production has not been as dramatic as in the case of opium during the same decade. Contrasting trends were recorded in various locations, including a long-term decline of use in North America but an increase in Europe, reductions in production in Colombia and increases in Peru or the Plurinational State of Bolivia. At the global level, these changes essentially amounted to geographical shifts and displacements in supply and demand. As a whole, the market has not been eliminated or significantly reduced over the last decade.

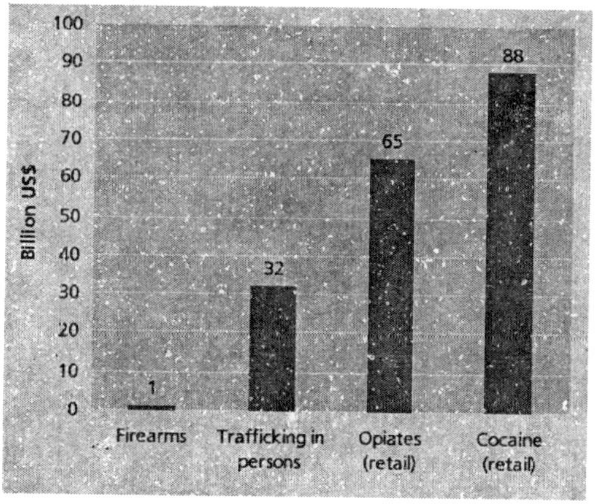

Figure 3. Estimated annual value of some global criminal markets in the 2000s

Data on cannabis and amphetamine-type stimulants are too patchy to allow year-on-year monitoring of the global market, but there were no indications of large reductions at the global level for these substances either. Member States have decided to continue their efforts to achieve the initial UNGASS objective. Accordingly, illicit drug supply and demand should be "eliminated or significantly reduced" by 2019. Their decision was made in a context of renewed criticism from some parts of civil society against the international drug control system and its perceived inefficacy, but governments were remarkably unanimous in their perception of the world drug problem, in the renewal of their political commitment to the international policy framework, and in their resolve to address shortcomings and obtain better results.

Can overall drug supply and demand be "eliminated or significantly reduced" by 2019, as called for by the Member States? At the national level, one can hope that many countries will be able to significantly improve their drug control situation within a decade. There are a number of encouraging developments in this respect. Will these local successes translate into an overall improvement at the global level?

The increase in world population alone (by some 0.8 billion people, or 11%) during the next decade should automatically increase the size of world drug markets, even if drug use prevalence rates remain constant. The potential impact of other risk factors such as urbanisation (+20% during the next decade) and the growth of megacities in the developing world could make matters worse, as drug use is typically higher in urban than in rural areas.

As regards cannabis, there is no global market per se to control and monitor. The global picture is made up of a patchwork of multiple and distinct submarkets, typically national or regional in nature. Monitoring their evolution and addressing them as a whole may thus neither be the easiest, nor necessarily the most useful, thing to do. Monitoring systems are largely missing, and current methods used to estimate the size and evolution of the global cannabis problems are not sensitive. That creates a serious technical problem for any attempt to closely monitor, guide and measure a global elimination approach. There are additional obstacles.

Cannabis production and consumption are found everywhere and there is no longer a clear consensus among national authorities on how to tackle the issue. Under these conditions, a significant reduction of the aggregate cannabis problem at the global level by 2019 would more likely be a matter of coincidence than the result of internationally concerted action. Even if such a reduction were to occur, it would be difficult to detect and reliably measure it, given the lack of a clear baseline and persistent data gaps.

Unlike for cannabis, there is a clear political consensus on heroin, cocaine and, to a large extent, amphetamines stimulants (ATS). In the case of ATS, because of the existence of independent, mostly regional or even national, supply and demand markets, as well as the ease, discretion and changing nature of synthetic drugs manufacture, the problem also tends to defy a global approach and overall predictions over the period considered.

Nevertheless, ATS have gained a large share of the global drug market over the last two decades and have come to represent a major and evolving threat for present and future drug control efforts. Since 1990, ATS manufacture has spread, with more than a third of Member States reporting this activity on their territory. Moreover, the global number of ATS users is likely to exceed the number of opiate and cocaine users combined.

These drugs require international vigilance, the adoption or strengthening of specific regulations and control measures at the global level, and the development of strong regional strategies is-by far-the most widely produced, seized and consumed drug worldwide, causing increased health problems in many countries, linked to its spread and rising potency in several (mostly developed) countries over the last decade. Deaths related to cannabis use are rare, however, and dependency tends to emerge only after long periods of use.

As cannabis production is widespread, most of its production is intended for local or regional consumption. Overseas trafficking in cannabis is less frequent and appears to have further lost importance with the development of high-potency cannabis production in greenhouses in the industrialised countries. The role of trans-national organised crime groups in the cannabis market is thus more limited than for other drugs, and so are the security threats related to its production, trafficking and consumption.

The global illicit opiate and cocaine markets represent two of the biggest trans-national drugs and crime threats of our time. Tens of thousands of the millions of opiate users worldwide die every year. Opiates are at the origin of two thirds of all drug treatment demand in Europe and Asia. The opiate market generates an annual turnover of up to US$65 billion, of which some US$ 55 billion for heroin alone.

Moreover, the opiate market is inter-linked with severe national and international security problems, particularly in Afghanistan and Pakistan. In terms of health impact, cocaine comes next, and represents as big a trans-national organised crime threat as heroin. Estimates suggest that the global retail sales figure (some US$88 billion) is even higher than for opiates, and the impact of the cocaine trade on stability can also be severe in some places.

The global heroin and cocaine markets appear simultaneously as persistent problems from a previous era of drug control, priorities for interventions due to the severity of their impacts on affected societies and good candidates for a global solution within a reasonable time-frame. Since they are both source from relatively concentrated production areas, most of their components are directly or indirectly linked. The resulting trans-national drug economies they form, from production to trafficking and consumption, can thus be addressed as a whole and be affected by shocks and ripple effects.

Not only are holistic market control approaches possible in these two cases, but, as shown by history, they are also a necessity. Local successes against illicit cultivation in the past–there were many– have always been offset by displacements to other locations, and closed trafficking routes replaced by new ones. Illicit production is presently largely entrenched in rural areas that are difficult to control. On the demand side, increases in cocaine consumption in Europe have tended to compensate reductions in North America, and the stabilisation of heroin use in West Europe has been offset by a deterioration of the situation in the Russian Federation. Meanwhile, the size and concentration of the trafficking flows to these main destination markets have often created havoc in vulnerable production and transit areas by overwhelming local law enforcement capacities, generating corruption, fuelling violence and instability, and spreading addiction. A clear lesson from the history of cocaine and heroin control is that the mere sum of uncoordinated national and sectorial efforts, even successful ones, cannot result in global success. Another lesson is that countries with limited means cannot resist, and counter the impact of, powerful trans-national trafficking flows on their own.

With the benefit of experience, success against these two markets appears to be within reach and would result in the removal of a large chunk of the world drug problem and many of its associated ills. As regards the availability of tools and data to guide interventions and monitor their impact, the situation is much better than in the case of other drugs. Production is already measured on a yearly basis and national data on trafficking is well reported by Member States. There is relatively good demand data from OECD countries, and gaps in other important consuming countries, particularly for heroin, could relatively easily be remedied by prevalence surveys for cocaine or by indirect measures, such as treatment multiplier methods, for heroin.

Global opium production and global coca production have grown by a factor of 6 (cocaine) and 7 (opium) during the last three decades. Eliminating or significantly reducing the world heroin and cocaine markets will thus require more effective approaches than in the past. What can be done? The first thing is to remedy the biggest shortcomings of previous approaches. Member States have recognised an essential one: a lack of integration. In the 2009 Political Declaration, Member States acknowledged "the importance of promoting, in order to enhance the effectiveness of drug control measures, an integrated approach in drug policies". This call is echoed in the new Plan of Action, notably in its Art. 27, under the title "Addressing supply and demand reduction together":

> "While drug trafficking is a multifaceted issue than can be effectively tackled only by reducing both supply and demand, this inter-linkage is often not taken into account."

To achieve the 2019 objectives, the international community needs to interweave drug supply and demand reduction interventions and integrate national efforts into the framework of renewed international strategies on the scale of the cocaine, heroin and ATS markets. To do so, it is urgent to improve our understanding of how these illicit trans-national drug economies operate.

Nature and Extent of Drug Use

Globally, UNODC estimates that between 155 and 250 million people, or 3.5% to 5.7% of the population aged 15-64, had used illicit substances at least once in the previous year. Cannabis users comprise the largest number of illicit drug users. Amphetamine-type stimulants are the second most commonly used illicit drugs, followed by opiates and cocaine.

However, in terms of harm associated with use, opiates would be ranked at the top. A comprehensive understanding of the extent of the drug use problem requires a review of several indicators the magnitude of drug use measured by prevalence (lifetime, annual, past 30 days) in the general population, the potential of problem drug use as measured by drug use among young people, and costs and consequences of drug use measured by treatment demand, drug-related morbidity and mortality. Additionally, to understand the dynamics of drug use in a country or region, it is important to look at the overall drug situation rather than merely the trends for individual drugs.

To illustrate, long-term trends in use of different drugs and overall drug use are presented for the United States of America, the United Kingdom, Australia and Spain where trend data over a longer period of time is available. Although short-term changes and trends might be observed in the use of different drugs, long-term trends suggest that the magnitude of the core of the problem does not change considerably in a few years. Indeed, to impact the drug use situation, long-term interventions for prevention of drug use and drug dependence treatment and care, along with supply reduction efforts, are required.

Problem Drug Use

At the core of drug use lie the problem drug users; those that might be regular or frequent users of the substances, considered dependent or injecting and who would have faced social and health consequences as a result of their drug use. Information on problem drug users from a policy and programme planning perspective is important as this drives the need and nature of the services required to address the diverse needs for treatment and care of drug dependent persons.

Lack of a global standard definition of a problem drug user One of the main challenges for UNODC remains the compilation of data reported by Member States and their comparability across countries and regions. The Commission on Narcotics Drugs in its forty-third session in 2000 endorsed the paper on 'Drug information systems: principles, structures and indicators' –also known as the 'Lisbon Consensus Document'. The document outlines the set of core epidemiological indicators to monitor the drug abuse situation, against which

Member States could report their respective situations through the Annual Reports Questionnaire (ARQ). One of the core indicators in the paper was 'high-risk drug consumption'. The assumption was that some drug information systems: principles, structures and indicators. Taking behaviours were particularly associated with severe problems and as such merit the attention of policymakers.

The document further elaborated that high-risk consumption included information on the number of drug injectors, estimates of daily users and those who are dependent. One challenge in measuring problem drug users or high-risk drug consumption is that most of these behaviours are hidden and have low prevalence. Therefore, they are poorly covered by general population estimates. Specific methods are required to gather information on such behaviours.

Out of the 110 Member States who responded to the 2008 ARQ on the extent and pattern of drug use, only 24 reported information on problem drug use. The definitions and methods of calculation differ from country to country. One country in Africa defines problem drug use as "drug users who constitute social harm and insecurity and drug users who relapse after rehabilitation." In North America, the DSM-IV3 defines the criteria for illicit drug dependence or abuse, while one country in Asia only considers heroin injectors as problem drug users.

The European Monitoring Centre for Drugs and Drug Addiction (EMCDDA), in its efforts to compile comparable information on problem drug use, defines it as "injecting drug use or long duration/regular use of ploidies, cocaine and/or amphetamines." The broad scope and differences in defining and understanding problem drug use in different regions signifies the need for setting common parameters, based on an already acceptable definition or criterion, for example, DSM-IV or ICD – 10, for determining, reporting and comparing the extent of harmful or high risk drug use at global level.

Number of Problem Drug Users is Stable

Based on the global estimates of cannabis, opiate, cocaine and amphetamine-type stimulant users, and using the relative risk coefficient, it is estimated that in 2008, there were between 16 and 38 million problem drug users (between 10%-15% of estimated drug users) in the world. The broad range of the estimate reflects the uncertainties in the available data globally.

In Europe, the prevalence rate of problem drug users varies between 2.7 in Greece and 9.0 in UK as rate per 1,000 population aged 15-64. The United Kingdom, Italy and Spain are on the higher end of the range, whereas Greece, Germany and Hungary are countries with low rates of problem drug use.

In the United States, million people-or 2.8% of the population aged 12 and older-were considered substance dependent, abusing illicit substances in 2008. Cannabis was the illicit substance with the highest rate of past year dependence, followed by pain relievers (ploidies) and cocaine. In Canada, 2.7% of the population aged 15 and older were reported to have experienced at least one type of harm in the past year due to illicit drug use. 'Harm' in the Canadian reports is classified as harm to physical health, or in the social, employment and legal spheres.

Injecting Drug Users (IDU)

Among the most problematic drug users are those who inject drugs. The last available estimate of the global number of IDU remains the one developed by the UNODC/UN AIDS reference group in 2008, which estimated that there are 15.9 million people who inject drugs (between 11 – 21.2

million). Of these, 3 million may be living with HIV (range 0.5-5.5 million). East Europe (1.5%) and Australia and New Zealand (1.03%) have a high prevalence of injecting drug use. In absolute numbers, East Europe has one of the highest numbers of injecting drug users. In East Europe most of the injectors are using opiates, while in Australia and New Zealand, methamphetamine is the main substance being injected.

Gap in Provision of Services to Problem Drug Users

The estimate of the global number of problem drug users provides the range of the number of people who need assistance to address their drug problems, including treatment of drug dependence and care. Comparing this with the number of people who are in treatment provides the magnitude of the unmet need for treatment of illicit drug use. Notwithstanding the gap in reporting and coverage of services, Member States reported that between 42% (in South America) and 5% (in Africa) of problem drug users were treated in the previous year. It can be estimated that globally, between 12% and 30% of problem drug users had received treatment in the past year, which means that between 11 million and 33.5 million problem drug users in the world have an unmet need for treatment interventions.

During the High-level Segment of the Commission on Narcotic Drugs in 2009, Member States adopted a Political Declaration and Plan of Action. The Plan of Action called for Member States to ensure that access to drug treatment is affordable, culturally appropriate and based on scientific evidence, and that drug dependence care services are included in the health care systems. It also called for the need to develop a comprehensive treatment system offering a wide range of integrated pharmacological (such as detoxification and opioid agonist and antagonist maintenance) and psychosocial (such as counselling, cognitive behavioural therapy and social support) interventions based on scientific evidence and focused on the process of rehabilitation, recovery and social reintegration.

The costs for the delivery of evidence-based treatment is seen to be much lower than the indirect costs caused by untreated drug dependence (prisons, unemployment, law enforcement and health consequences). Research indicates that spending on treatment produces savings in terms of a reduction in the number of crime victims, as well as reduced expenditures for the criminal justice system. At a minimum there was a 3:1 savings rate, and when a broader calculation of costs associated with crime, health and social productivity was taken into account, the rate of savings to investment rose to 13:1.

These savings can improve disadvantaged situations where opportunities for education, employment and social welfare are undermined, and increase possibilities for families to recover battered economies, thus facilitating social and economic development. Trends in the main drugs of concern in problem drug users as indicated by treatment demand. An analysis of the number of treatment services provided in a country according to the main drug for admission can provide information on the drugs that are most problematic in terms of health and social consequences and need for intervention.

The treatment demand data presented here cover the 10-year period from the late 1990s to 2008. Data for all but 2008 were published in the World Drug Report 2000 and WDR 2005 through 2009. The data show that there is generally, in each region, a clear, and over the past 10 years consistent, drug type that dominates treatment. This suggests marked regional differences in the drugs that affect problem drug users. Indeed, in the last decade, the primary drug for treatment has remained cannabis in Africa, cocaine in South

America and opiates in Asia and Europe. The two notable exceptions are:

— North America, where a dominant drug for treatment demand does not emerge, and rather, the percentage breakdown of drugs has become more uniform over time.

— Oceania, which has experienced over time one of the biggest changes in the primary treatment drug from opiates to cannabis.

The changes observed over the last decade in the contribution that each drug has made to treatment admissions suggest an ongoing diversification of problem drug users in some regions. The contribution of cannabis to treatment demand is increasing in Europe, South America and Oceania, while admissions for synthetic opiates in North America sharply increased in the last few years, compensating for decreased admissions for heroin. In Europe, the admissions for stimulants (cocaine and amphetamine-type stimulants) and cannabis have also increased over time, in parallel with a decline in admissions for opiates.

Interpreting trends in treatment demand data is challenging as patterns and trends over time can reflect a mixture of factors, such as:

— The development and improved coverage of drug treatment reporting systems.

— Statistical artefacts, for example, resulting from different countries reporting in a region in different time periods (notably in Africa).

— Changing patterns of consumption including prevalence, frequency of drug use and the typical amounts used on each occasion.

— Prevention measures and the availability, accessibility and utilisation of treatment services;

— Response of the criminal justice system to drug offenders, such as compulsory treatment as an alternative to imprisonment.

Opiates

Opiates are clearly the main problem drug as indicated by treatment demand over the past 10 years in Europe (with at least 55% of demand) and Asia.

Opiates have also increased their contribution in Africa from 8% to 20%. While there has been an increase in opiate-related treatment in Africa over the last decade, the strong increase is, however, to some extent, a statistical artefact as previous treatment data (dating back more than 10 years) were removed and could not be replaced as no new data were forthcoming. Therefore, data from smaller island countries - such as Mauritius or the Seychelles, where the proportion of opiate treatment has historically been very high - contribute more to the treatment demand for opiates in Africa.

Opiate-related treatment has recently exhibited a large increase in North America, from 10% to 23%, reflecting the rising abuse of synthetic ploidies, and are possibly starting to emerge in South America. Oceania has experienced a striking decline in the contribution of opiates to treatment demand from 66% to 26%, in line with the severe heroin shortage of 2001 in Australia which convinced many heroin addicts to give up their habit.

Synthetic Opioids

Treatment demand data from the United States of America and Canada both show an increase of problem drug users linked to the use of synthetic opioids/ prescription medicine and a decline in the heroin-related problem users. In the United States, admissions where opiates were the primary drug of concern increased by 34% between 1997 and 2007 (typically representing 29-32% of demand for treatment, excluding alcohol). Heroin is still the major contributor to the treatment demand for opioids, but this has become less marked with the steady increase in demand for treatment for synthetic opioids.

The contribution of heroin to opioid admissions has continually declined from 94% to 73%, with the number of admissions for heroin starting to decline in 2002. In contrast, the number of admissions for other opiates/synthetic opioids has increased from, 274 to 90,516 between 1997 and 2007, from contributing just 6% of opioid admissions in 1997 to 27% in 2007. A similar situation is found in Canada. Treatment demand for prescription opioids has been greater than for heroin/ opium over the past few years, and it is still increasing.

Treatment demand data from Ontario show that the number of admissions for opioids increased 55% between 2004/2005 and 2008/2009, or from 14.7% to 18.5% of all drug treatment demand (excluding alcohol and tobacco). This increase is attributable to the 68% rise in admissions for prescription opioids/codeine. The contribution of prescription opioids/codeine to all admissions (excluding alcohol and tobacco) has increased from 12.1% to 16.5%, while the heroin/opium contribution has declined from 2.6% to 2.0%.

Cannabis

Although it is the world's most widely used drug, cannabis is often thought to be the least harmful and of little interest to public health, in spite of the fact that evidence in recent years has shown that the use of cannabis can create remarkable levels of harm. Data on treatment demand for cannabis and medical research have pointed to the potentially severe health consequences of cannabis use.

The most probable adverse effects of cannabis use include dependency, increased risk of motor vehicle accidents, impaired respiratory function, cardiovascular disease and adverse effects of regular use on adolescent psychosocial development and mental health. The rising number of cannabis-related problem drug users is often not correlated with a similar rise in the overall number of cannabis users, suggesting that the risks associated with the use of cannabis have been increasingly recognised and diagnosed in recent years. Rising levels in cannabis potency in many parts of the world have also contributed to the increased risk of cannabis use.

Cannabis is clearly the dominant drug for treatment in Africa with consistently over 60% of demand. Over the past 10 years, cannabis has been making an increasing contribution to treatment demand in Europe, South America and Oceania. Only North America has seen a reduction in the contribution of cannabis to treatment demand compared to other drugs.

Treatment episodes where cannabis was the primary drug of concern increased in Australia by 34%, from 23,826 to 31,864 between 2002 and 2008 alone, despite a sharp decline in cannabis use among the general population. Possible explanations for the increasing trend in the problematic use of cannabis and cannabis-related harm include:

> increased consumption among older users reflecting dependence among those who have had a long history of use that was initiated at a relatively young age; and the increased availability of cheaper and possibly higher potency cannabis. Referrals from the criminal justice system do not seem to have had an influence on the increase in the numbers entering treatment in Australia.

Contributing factors for increasing treatment demand for cannabis in Europe remain uncertain Cannabis ranks second for treatment demand at the European level and its contribution to drug treatment demand has been steadily increasing. The EMCDDA has been documenting rising levels of demand for treatment from cannabis-related problems since 1996, but there are wide discrepancies between countries. In 2006, 21% of all European clients and 28% of new clients entered treatment with cannabis as the primary drug of concern. In Denmark, Germany, France, Hungary and Turkey the percentage of new clients seeking treatment for cannabis as the primary drug was greater than 50%.

However, reasons for the increase in demand have proved difficult to identify and EMCDDA recommends further research to tackle this issue. The effect of poly-drug use in the treatment statistics should not be disregarded. While drug treatment seekers in the past may have been registered almost automatically for heroin, they may now be more accurately registered as having cannabis as the primary problem drug while consuming other drugs as well. Moreover, the increasing complexity of drug use makes it difficult to have a simple characterisation of problem drug users according to a single drug type. In the context of drug users combining the use of different drugs to get the effect they want to achieve, the use of cannabis becomes potentially more harmful because its effect combined with other drugs can be very different from when it is used alone.

Cocaine is the main problem drug in the Americas, but its contribution is declining in North America Treatment demand for cocaine is most dominant in the Americas, where coca cultivation is concentrated. Cocaine is the main problem drug according to treatment demand for South America, and where once it appeared to be on the decline, over the last few years, the situation has stabilised.

Although cocaine was the main drug for treatment in North America in the late 1990s, the cocaine-related treatment demand has been declining over the last decade, and was responsible for just 31% of total treatment demand in 2008. In Europe, the treatment demand, in contrast, increased from 3% to 10% over the same period. Cocaine-related treatment demand in Africa accounts for less than 10% of the total, and in Asia and Oceania demand is negligible.

Asia has the highest percentage of admissions for amphetamine-type stimulants (ATS), where it ranks as the second most important drug. In Oceania and North America, treatment demand for ATS has increased to some 20% since the late 1990s. Otherwise, demand for treatment has remained below approximately 10% in other regions, with a possible recent emergence in South America. It should be noted that treatment for ATS is often administered differently than for other drugs, and can be easily under-reported.

6

Problem of Mental Illness

Mental disorder or mental illness is a psychological or behavioral pattern associated with distress or disability that occurs in an individual and is not a part of normal development or culture. The recognition and understanding of mental health conditions has changed over time and across cultures, and there are still variations in the definition, assessment, and classification of mental disorders, although standard guideline criteria are widely accepted.

Currently, mental disorders are conceptualized as disorders of brain circuits likely caused by developmental processes shaped by a complex interplay of genetics and experience. In other words, the genetics of mental illness may really be the genetics of brain development, with different outcomes possible, depending on the biological and environmental context.

Over a third of people in most countries report meeting criteria for the major categories at some point in their life. The causes are often explained in terms of a diathesis-stress model and biopsychosocial model. Services are based in psychiatric hospitals or in the community. Diagnoses are made by psychiatrists or clinical psychologists using various methods, often relying on observation and questioning in interviews. Treatments are provided by various mental health professionals.

Psychotherapy and psychiatric medication are two major treatment options as are social interventions, peer support and self-help. In some cases there may be involuntary detention and involuntary treatment where legislation allows. Stigma and discrimination add to the suffering associated with the disorders, and have led to various social movements campaign for change.

Problems associated with people with mental illness pose a significant challenge for modern policing. This guide begins by describing the problem and reviewing factors that increase the challenges that police face in relation to the mentally ill. It then identifies a series of questions that might help you analyse your local policing problems associated with people with mental illness. Finally, it reviews responses to the problems and what we know about these from evaluative research and police practice.

Over the last decade, many police agencies have sought to improve their response to incidents involving people with mental illness, especially emergency mental health situations. These new developments, however, have been targeted almost exclusively at improved handling of individual incidents. Little attention has been devoted to developing or implementing a comprehensive and preventive approach to the issue.

Classifications

The definition and classification of mental disorders is a key issue for mental health and for users and providers of mental health services. Most international clinical documents use the term "mental disorder". There are currently two widely established systems that classify mental disorders—*ICD-10 Chapter V: Mental and behavioural disorders*, part of the International Classification of Diseases produced by the World Health Organization (WHO), and the *Diagnostic and*

Statistical Manual of Mental Disorders (DSM-IV) produced by the American Psychiatric Association (APA). Both list categories of disorder and provide standardized criteria for diagnosis. They have deliberately converged their codes in recent revisions so that the manuals are often broadly comparable, although significant differences remain. Other classification schemes may be used in non-western cultures (see, for example, the *Chinese Classification of Mental Disorders*), and other manuals may be used by those of alternative theoretical persuasions, for example the *Psychodynamic Diagnostic Manual*. In general, mental disorders are classified separately to neurological disorders, learning disabilities or mental retardation.

Unlike most of the above systems, some approaches to classification do not employ distinct categories of disorder or dichotomous cut-offs intended to separate the abnormal from the normal. There is significant scientific debate about the different kinds of categorization and the relative merits of categorical versus non-categorical (or hybrid) schemes, with the latter including spectrum, continuum or dimensional systems.

There are many different categories of mental disorder, and many different facets of human behavior and personality that can become disordered.

Anxiety or fear that interferes with normal functioning may be classified as an anxiety disorder. Commonly recognized categories include specific phobias, generalized anxiety disorder, social anxiety disorder, panic disorder, agoraphobia, obsessive-compulsive disorder and post-traumatic stress disorder.

Other affective (emotion/mood) processes can also become disordered. Mood disorder involving unusually intense and sustained sadness, melancholia or despair is known as Major depression or Clinical depression (milder but still prolonged depression can be diagnosed as dysthymia). Bipolar disorder (also known as manic depression) involves abnormally "high" or pressured mood states, known as mania or hypomania, alternating with normal or depressed mood. Whether unipolar and bipolar mood phenomena represent distinct categories of disorder, or whether they usually mix and merge together along a dimension or spectrum of mood, is under debate in the scientific literature.

Patterns of belief, language use and perception can become disordered (e.g. delusions, thought disorder, hallucinations). Psychotic disorders in this domain include schizophrenia, and delusional disorder. Schizoaffective disorder is a category used for individuals showing aspects of both schizophrenia and affective disorders. Schizotypy is a category used for individuals showing some of the characteristics associated with schizophrenia but without meeting cut-off criteria.

Personality—the fundamental characteristics of a person that influence his or her thoughts and behaviors across situations and time—may be considered disordered if judged to be abnormally rigid and maladaptive. Categorical schemes list a number of different such personality disorders, including those sometimes classed as eccentric (e.g. paranoid, schizoid and schizotypal personality disorders), to those sometimes classed as dramatic or emotional (antisocial, borderline, histrionic or narcissistic personality disorders) or those seen as fear-related (avoidant, dependent, or obsessive-compulsive personality disorders). If an inability to sufficiently adjust to life circumstances begins within three months of a particular event or situation, and ends within six months after the stressor stops or is eliminated, it may instead be classed as an adjustment disorder. There is an emerging consensus that so-called "personality disorders", like personality traits in general, actually incorporate a mixture of acute dysfunctional behaviors that resolve in short periods, and maladaptive temperamental traits that are more stable. Furthermore, there are also non-categorical schemes that rate all individuals via a profile of different dimensions of personality rather than using a cut-off from normal personality variation, for example through schemes based on the Big Five personality traits.

Eating disorders involve disproportionate concern in matters of food and weight. Categories of disorder in this area include anorexia nervosa, bulimia nervosa, exercise bulimia or binge eating disorder.

Sleep disorders such as insomnia involve disruption to normal sleep patterns, or a feeling of tiredness despite sleep appearing normal.

Sexual and gender identity disorders may be diagnosed, including dyspareunia, gender identity disorder and ego-dystonic homosexuality. Various kinds of paraphilia are considered mental disorders (sexual arousal to objects, situations, or individuals that are considered abnormal or harmful to the person or others).

People who are abnormally unable to resist certain urges or impulses that could be harmful to themselves or others, may be classed as having an impulse control disorder, including various kinds of tic disorders such as Tourette's syndrome, and disorders such as kleptomania (stealing) or pyromania (fire-setting). Various behavioral addictions, such as gambling addiction, may be classed as a disorder. Obsessive-compulsive disorder can sometimes involve an inability to resist certain acts but is classed separately as being primarily an anxiety disorder.

The use of drugs (legal or illegal), when it persists despite significant problems related to the use, may be defined as a mental disorder termed substance dependence or substance abuse (a broader category than drug abuse). The DSM does not currently use the common term drug addiction and the ICD simply talks about "harmful use". Disordered substance use may be due to a pattern of compulsive and repetitive use of the drug that results in tolerance to its effects and withdrawal symptoms when use is reduced or stopped.

People who suffer severe disturbances of their self-identity, memory and general awareness of themselves and their surroundings may be classed as having a dissociative identity disorder, such as depersonalization disorder or Dissociative Identity Disorder itself (which has also been called multiple personality disorder, or "split personality"). Other memory or cognitive disorders include amnesia or various kinds of old age dementia.

A range of developmental disorders that initially occur in childhood may be diagnosed, for example autism spectrum disorders, oppositional defiant disorder and conduct disorder, and attention deficit hyperactivity disorder (ADHD), which may continue into adulthood.

Conduct disorder, if continuing into adulthood, may be diagnosed as antisocial personality disorder (dissocial personality disorder in the ICD). Popularist labels such as psychopath (or sociopath) do not appear in the DSM or ICD but are linked by some to these diagnoses.

Disorders appearing to originate in the body, but thought to be mental, are known as somatoform disorders, including somatization disorder and conversion disorder. There are also disorders of the perception of the body, including body dysmorphic disorder. Neurasthenia is an old diagnosis involving somatic complaints as well as fatigue and low spirits/depression, which is officially recognized by the ICD-10 but no longer by the DSM-IV.

Factitious disorders, such as Munchausen syndrome, are diagnosed where symptoms are thought to be experienced (deliberately produced) and/or reported (feigned) for personal gain.

There are attempts to introduce a category of relational disorder, where the diagnosis is of a relationship rather than on any one individual in that relationship. The relationship may be between children and their parents, between couples, or others. There already exists, under the category of psychosis, a diagnosis of shared psychotic disorder where two or more individuals share a particular delusion because of their close relationship with each other.

Various new types of mental disorder diagnosis are occasionally proposed. Among those controversially considered by the official committees of the diagnostic manuals include self-defeating personality disorder, sadistic personality disorder, passive-aggressive personality disorder and premenstrual dysphoric disorder.

Two recent unique isolated proposals are solastalgia by Glenn Albrecht and hubris syndrome by David Owen. The application of the concept of mental illness to the phenomena described by these authors has in turn been critiqued by Seamus Mac Suibhne.

Dangerousness

Police officers encounter people with mental illness in many different types of situations, in roles that include criminal offenders, disorderly persons, missing persons, complainants, victims, and persons in need of care. According to one Texas study, the five most frequent scenarios are as follows:

— A family member, friend, or other concerned person calls the police for help during a psychiatric emergency.

— A person with mental illness feels suicidal and calls the police as a cry for help.

— Police officers encounter a person with mental illness behaving inappropriately in public.

— Citizens call the police because they feel threatened by the unusual behaviour or the mere presence of a person with mental illness.

— A person with mental illness calls the police for help because of imagined threats.

Of these typical situations, ones involving the threat of suicide were rated as the most difficult to handle. Each of the others listed above was rated as somewhat difficult to handle. The two behaviours that were rated as most problematic overall were threatening suicide and nuisance behaviours.

These are the most common situations in which police encounter people with mental illness. It is important to realise, though, that when police officers handle some of these situations they do not always realise that mental illness is involved (such as a shoplifting or a disorderly person). Officers may try to handle the situation as usual (by giving directions, issuing commands, or making an arrest, for example) but not get the cooperation or compliance expected, sometimes leading to escalating tension. This highlights the importance of training in mental illness recognition as well as crisis management techniques.

A fairly common perception is that people with mental illness are disproportionately involved in violent crime. This is true in one respect but not in another. A small subset of people with mental illness, those who are actively experiencing serious psychotic symptoms, are more violent than the general population. Research suggests several factors associated with this group's violent behaviour, including drug and alcohol abuse, noncompliance with medication requirements, and biological or biochemical disorders. In general, however, "violent and criminal acts directly attributable to mental illness account for a very small proportion of all such acts in the United States.

Most persons with mental illness are not criminals, and of those who are, most are not violent." Police interactions with people with mental illness can be dangerous, but usually are not. In the United States, 982 of 58,066 police officers assaulted in 2002, and 15 of 636 police officers feloniously killed from 1993 to 2002, had "mentally deranged" assailants. These represent one out of every 59 assaults on officers and one out of every 42 The Problem of People with Mental Illness officers feloniously killed—relatively small portions of all officers assaulted and killed.

Encounters with police are more likely to be dangerous for people with mental illness than for the police. An early study found that an average of nine New York City police shootings per year between 1971 and 1975 involved emotionally disturbed people. Between 1994 and 1999, Los Angeles officers shot 37 people during encounters with people with mental illness, killing 25. A review of shootings by the police from 1998 to 2001 in the United Kingdom indicated that almost half involved someone with a known history of mental health problems. It is estimated that people with severe mental illness are four times more likely to be killed by police. Serious injury and death of people with mental illness at the hands of the police are especially tragic, for obvious reasons. Reduction of such injuries and deaths should be a high-priority objective for every police agency.

The harms associated with the police handling of people with mental illness are implicit in the situations and examples the table provides, but deserve some discussion. A person with mental illness may harm other citizens by committing personal or property crimes or engaging in disorderly and disruptive behaviour. Alternatively, a person with mental illness may be harmed as a crime victim, as an abused family member or patient, as a person who suffers through self-neglect, or as a person whose mental health problem has left him or her erroneously subjected to criminal charges and jail confinement. Society in general may be harmed if excessive police, criminal justice, and/or medical resources are consumed by problems associated with people with mental illness.

It is important to keep the concept of harm in mind when addressing this particular problem, because there is a tendency to simply define people with mental illness as the problem, and getting them out of sight as the solution. In contrast to most police problems, however, this is not one that involves wholly voluntary behaviour—rather, it involves behaviour that medical conditions cause or compound. Consequently, police have to be careful not to blame people with mental illness, but instead focus on behaviour that causes harm to self or others.

The police problem of people with mental illness is closely connected to three other problems noted below. This guide does not specifically address these problems, but addressing people with mental illness in your jurisdiction may require that you take on these problems, as well:

— Homelessness.

— Drug abuse.

— Alcohol abuse.

The people the police encounter who have mental health problems or emergencies are also frequently homeless. For example, a Honolulu study found that 74 percent of law violators who the police believed to have a mental disorder were also homeless. In London, about 30 percent of minor offenders referred for admission to a station-house diversion program for the "mentally disordered" were living on the streets.

Similarly, the people with mental illness the police encounter are likely to have substance abuse problems. About three-quarters of jail and prison inmates with mental illness also have a substance abuse problem. Current substance abuse was identified for about half of psychiatric emergency room referrals in New York State, and nearly two-thirds of psychiatric emergency patients evaluated by a police-mental health out reach team in Los Angeles were known to be serious substance abusers.

Causes of Mental Ddisorders

Mental disorders can arise from a combination of sources. In many cases there is no single accepted or consistent cause currently established. A common belief even to this day is that disorders result from genetic vulnerabilities exposed by environmental stressors. However, it is clear enough from a simple statistical analysis across the whole spectrum of mental health disorders at least in western cultures that there is a strong relationship between the various forms of severe and complex mental disorder in adulthood and the abuse (physical, sexual or emotional) or neglect of children during the developmental years. Child sexual abuse alone plays a significant role in the causation of a significant percentage of all mental disorders in adult females, most notable examples being eating disorders and borderline personality disorder.

An eclectic or pluralistic mix of models may be used to explain particular disorders, and the primary paradigm of contemporary mainstream Western psychiatry is said to be the biopsychosocial (BPS) model, incorporating biological, psychological and social factors, although this may not always be applied in practice. Biopsychiatry has tended to follow a biomedical model, focusing on "organic" or "hardware" pathology of the brain. Psychoanalytic theories have continued to evolve alongside congitive-behavioural and systemic-family approaches been popular but are now less so. Evolutionary psychology may be used as an overall explanatory theory, and attachment theory is another kind of evolutionary-psychological approach sometimes applied in the context of mental disorders. A distinction is sometimes made between a "medical model" or a "social model" of disorder and disability.

Studies have indicated that genes often play an important role in the development of mental disorders, although the reliable identification of connections between specific genes and specific categories of disorder has proven more difficult. Environmental events surrounding pregnancy and birth have also been implicated. Traumatic brain injury may increase the risk of developing certain mental disorders. There have been some tentative inconsistent links found to certain viral infections, to substance misuse, and to general physical health.

Abnormal functioning of neurotransmitter systems has been implicated, including serotonin, norepinephrine, dopamine and glutamate systems. Differences have also been found in the size or activity of certain brain regions in some cases. Psychological mechanisms have also been implicated, such as cognitive (e.g. reason), emotional processes, personality, temperament and coping style.

Social influences have been found to be important, including abuse, bullying and other negative or stressful life experiences. The specific risks and pathways to particular disorders are less clear, however. Aspects of the wider community have also been implicated, including employment problems, socioeconomic inequality, lack of social cohesion, problems linked to migration, and features of particular societies and cultures.

Gender-specific indicators of mental illness incorporate physical or sexual abuse, stress, loss of social network, rape and domestic violence, high progesterone oral contraceptives, and mood disorders during early reproductive years . It is important to note that the intersection of biological, social, and behavioral health problems may result in exacerbated mental health issues. The disproportionate effects of these issues on women's lives limit their coping skills, leading to negative behaviors such as substance abuse. Finally, these circumstances improve the risk of poor physical health, anxiety, and depression.

Management and Treatment

Treatment and support for mental disorders is provided in psychiatric hospitals, clinics or any of a diverse range of community mental health services. In many countries services are increasingly based on a recovery model that is meant to support each individual's independence, choice and personal journey to regain a meaningful life, although individuals may be treated against their will in a minority of cases. There are a range of different types of treatment and what is most suitable depends on the disorder and on the individual. Many things have been found to help at least some people, and a placebo effect may play a role in any intervention or medication.

A major option for many mental disorders is psychotherapy. There are several main types. Cognitive behavioral therapy (CBT) is widely used and is based on modifying the patterns of thought and behavior associated with a particular disorder. Psychoanalysis, addressing underlying psychic conflicts and defenses, has been a dominant school of psychotherapy and is still in use. Systemic therapy or family therapy is sometimes used, addressing a network of significant others as well as an individual. Some psychotherapies are based on a humanistic approach. There are a number of specific therapies used for particular disorders, which may be offshoots or hybrids of the above types. Mental health professionals often employ an eclectic or integrative approach. Much may depend on the therapeutic relationship, and there may be problems with trust, confidentiality and engagement.

A major option for many mental disorders is psychiatric medication and there are several main groups. Antidepressants are used for the treatment of clinical depression as well as often for anxiety and other disorders. Anxiolytics are used for anxiety disorders and related problems such as insomnia. Mood stabilizers are used primarily in bipolar disorder. Antipsychotics are mainly used for psychotic disorders, notably for positive symptoms in schizophrenia. Stimulants are commonly used, notably for ADHD.

Despite the different conventional names of the drug groups, there may be considerable overlap in the disorders for which they are actually indicated, and there may also be off-label use of medications. There can be problems with adverse effects of medication and adherence to them, and there is also criticism of pharmaceutical marketing and professional conflicts of interest.

Electroconvulsive therapy (ECT) is sometimes used in severe cases when other interventions for severe intractable depression have failed. Psychosurgery is considered experimental but is advocated by certain neurologists in certain rare cases.

Counseling (professional) and co-counseling (between peers) may be used. Psychoeducation programs may provide people with the information to understand and manage their problems. Creative therapies are sometimes used, including music therapy, art therapy or drama therapy. Lifestyle adjustments and supportive measures are often used, including peer support, self-help groups for mental health and supported housing or supported employment (including social firms). Some advocate dietary supplements.

Prognosis depends on the disorder, the individual and numerous related factors. Some disorders are transient, while others may last a lifetime. Some disorders may be very limited in their functional effects, while others may involve substantial disability and support needs. The degree of ability or disability may vary across different life domains. Continued disability has been linked to institutionalization, discrimination and social exclusion as well as to the inherent properties of disorders.

Even those disorders often considered the most serious and intractable have varied courses. Long-term international studies of schizophrenia have found that over a half of individuals recover in terms of symptoms, and around a fifth to a third in terms of symptoms and functioning, with some requiring no medication. At the same time, many have serious difficulties and support needs for many years, although "late" recovery is still possible. The World Health Organization concluded that the long-term studies' findings converged with others in "relieving patients, carers and clinicians of the chronicity paradigm which dominated thinking throughout much of the 20th century." Around half of people initially diagnosed with bipolar disorder achieve syndromal recovery (no longer meeting criteria for the diagnosis) within six weeks, and nearly all achieve it within two years, with nearly half regaining their prior occupational and residential status in that period. However, nearly half go on to experience a new episode of mania or major depression within the next two years. Functioning has been found to vary, being poor during periods of major depression or mania but otherwise fair to good, and possibly superior during periods of hypomania in Bipolar II.

Despite often being characterized in purely negative terms, some mental states labeled as disorders can also involve above-average creativity, non-conformity, goal-striving, meticulousness, or empathy. In addition, the public perception of the level of disability associated with mental disorders can change.

PREVALENCE OF MENTAL DISORDERS

Mental disorders are common. World wide more than one in three people in most countries report sufficient criteria for at least one at some point in their life. In the United States 46% qualifies for a mental illness at some point. An ongoing survey indicates that anxiety disorders are the most common in all but one country, followed by mood disorders in all but two countries, while substance disorders and impulse-control disorders were consistently less prevalent. Rates varied by region. Such statistics are widely believed to be underestimates, due to poor diagnosis (especially in countries without affordable access to mental health services) and low reporting rates, in part because of the predominant use of self-report data rather than semi-structured instruments. Actual lifetime prevalence rates for mental disorders are estimated to be between 65% and 85%.

A review of anxiety disorder surveys in different countries found average lifetime prevalence estimates of 16.6%, with women having higher rates on average. A review of mood disorder surveys in different countries found lifetime rates of 6.7% for major depressive disorder (higher in some studies, and in women) and 0.8% for Bipolar I disorder.

In the United States the frequency of disorder is: anxiety disorder (28.8%), mood disorder (20.8%), impulse-control disorder (24.8%) or substance use disorder (14.6%).

A 2004 cross-Europe study found that approximately one in four people reported meeting criteria at some point in their life for at least one of the DSM-IV disorders assessed, which included mood disorders (13.9%), anxiety disorders (13.6%) or alcohol disorder (5.2%). Approximately one in ten met criteria within a 12-month period. Women and younger people of either gender showed more cases of disorder. A 2005 review of surveys in 16 European countries found that 27% of adult Europeans are affected by at least one mental disorder in a 12 month period.

An international review of studies on the prevalence of schizophrenia found an average (median) figure of 0.4% for lifetime prevalence; it was consistently lower in poorer countries.

Studies of the prevalence of personality disorders (PDs) have been fewer and smaller-scale, but one broad Norwegian survey found a five-year prevalence of almost 1 in 7 (13.4%). Rates for specific disorders ranged from 0.8% to 2.8%, differing across countries, and by gender, educational level and other factors. A US survey that incidentally screened for personality disorder found a rate of 14.79%.

Approximately 7% of a preschool pediatric sample were given a psychiatric diagnosis in one clinical study, and approximately 10% of 1- and 2-year-olds receiving developmental screening have been assessed as having significant emotional/behavioral problems based on parent and pediatrician reports.

While rates of psychological disorders are the same for men and women, women have twice the rate of depression than men . Each year 73 million women are afflicted with **major depression**, and suicide is ranked 7th as the cause of death for women between the ages of 20-59. Depressive disorders account for close to 41.9% of the disability from neuropsychiatric disorders among women compared to 29.3% among men. .

Imapcts on Society and Culture

Different societies or cultures and even different individuals in a culture can disagree as to what constitutes optimal versus pathological biological and psychological functioning. Research has demonstrated that cultures vary in the relative importance placed on, for example, happiness, autonomy, or social relationships for pleasure. Likewise, the fact that a behavior pattern is valued, accepted, encouraged, or even statistically normative in a culture does not necessarily mean that it is conducive to optimal psychological functioning.

People in all cultures find some behaviors bizarre or even incomprehensible. But just what they feel is bizarre or incomprehensible is ambiguous and subjective. These differences in determination can become highly contentious.

The process by which conditions and difficulties come to be defined and treated as medical conditions and problems, and thus come under the authority of doctors and other health professionals, is known as medicalization or pathologization.

In the scientific and academic literature on the definition or classification of mental disorder, one extreme argues that it is entirely a matter of value judgements (including of what is normal) while another proposes that it is or could be entirely objective and scientific (including by reference to statistical norms). Common hybrid views argue that the concept of mental disorder is objective but a "fuzzy prototype" that can never be precisely defined, or alternatively that it inevitably involves a mix of scientific facts and subjective value judgments.

A number of professions have developed that specialize in the treatment of mental disorders, including the medical speciality of psychiatry (including psychiatric nursing), a subset of psychology known as clinical psychology, social work, as well as mental health counselors, marriage and family therapists, psychotherapists, counselors and public health professionals. Those with personal experience of using mental health services are also increasingly involved in researching and delivering mental health services and working as mental health professionals. The different clinical and scientific perspectives draw on diverse fields of research and theory, and different disciplines may favor differing models, explanations and goals.

Religious, spiritual, or transpersonal experiences and beliefs are typically not defined as disordered, especially if widely shared, despite meeting many criteria of delusional or psychotic disorders. Even when a belief or experience can be shown to produce distress or disability—the ordinary standard for judging mental disorders—the presence of a strong cultural basis for that belief, experience, or interpretation of experience, generally disqualifies it from counting as evidence of mental disorder.

Current diagnostic guidelines have been criticized as having a fundamentally Euro-American outlook. They have been widely implemented, but opponents argue that even when diagnostic criteria are accepted across different cultures, it does not mean that the underlying constructs have any validity within those cultures; even reliable application can prove only consistency, not legitimacy.

Advocating a more culturally sensitive approach, critics such as Carl Bell and Marcello Maviglia contend that the cultural and ethnic diversity of individuals is often discounted by researchers and service providers.

Cross-cultural psychiatrist Arthur Kleinman contends that the Western bias is ironically illustrated in the introduction of cultural factors to the DSM-IV: that disorders or concepts from non-Western or non-mainstream cultures are described as "culture-bound", whereas standard psychiatric diagnoses are given no cultural qualification whatsoever, reveals to Kleinman an underlying assumption that Western cultural phenomena are universal. Kleinman's negative view towards the culture-bound syndrome is largely shared by other cross-cultural critics, common responses included both disappointment over the large number of documented non-Western mental disorders still left out and frustration that even those included were often misinterpreted or misrepresented.

Many mainstream psychiatrists are dissatisfied with the new culture-bound diagnoses, although for different reasons. Robert Spitzer, a lead architect of the DSM-III, has hypothesized that adding cultural formulations was an attempt to appease cultural critics and stated that the formulations lack any scientific motivation or support. Spitzer also posits that the new culture-bound diagnoses are rarely used, maintaining that the standard diagnoses apply regardless of the culture involved. In general, mainstream psychiatric opinion remains that if a diagnostic category is valid, cross-cultural factors are either irrelevant or are significant only to specific symptom presentations.

Clinical conceptions of mental illness also overlap with personal and cultural values in the domain of morality, so much so that it is sometimes argued that separating the two is impossible without fundamentally redefining the essence of being a particular person in a society. In clinical psychiatry, persistent distress and disability indicate an internal disorder requiring treatment; but in another context, that same distress and disability can be seen as an indicator of emotional struggle and the need to address social and structural problems. This dichotomy has lead some academics and clinicians to advocate a postmodernist conceptualization of mental distress and well-being.

Such approaches, along with cross-cultural and "heretical" psychologies centered on alternative cultural and ethnic and race-based identities and experiences, stand in contrast to the mainstream psychiatric community's active avoidance of any involvement with either morality or culture. In many countries there are attempts to challenge perceived prejudice against minority groups, including alleged institutional racism within psychiatric services.

Three quarters of countries around the world have mental health legislation. Compulsory admission to mental health facilities (also known as involuntary commitment or sectioning), is a controversial topic. From some points of view it can impinge on personal liberty and the right to choose, and carry the risk of abuse for political, social and other reasons; from other points of view, it can potentially prevent harm to self and others, and assist some people in attaining their right to healthcare when unable to decide in their own interests.

All human-rights oriented mental health laws require proof of the presence of a mental disorder as defined by internationally accepted standards, but the type and severity of disorder that counts can vary in different jurisdictions. The two most often utilized grounds for involuntary admission are said to be serious likelihood of immediate or imminent danger to self or others, and the need for treatment. Applications for someone to be involuntarily admitted may usually come from a mental health practitioner, a family member, a close relative, or a guardian. Human-rights-oriented laws usually stipulate that independent medical practitioners or other accredited mental health practitioners must examine the patient separately and that there should be regular, time-bound review by an independent review body. An individual must be shown to lack the capacity to give or withhold informed consent (i.e. to understand treatment information and its implications). Legal challenges in some areas have resulted in supreme court decisions that a person does *not* have to agree with a psychiatrist's characterization of their issues as an "illness", nor with a psychiatrist's conviction in medication, but only recognize the issues and the information about treatment options.

Proxy consent (also known as substituted decision-making) may be given to a personal representative, a family member or a legally appointed guardian, or patients may have been able to enact an advance directive as to how they wish to be treated. The right to supported decision-making may also be included in legislation. Involuntary treatment laws are increasingly extended to those living in the community, for example outpatient commitment laws (known by different names) are used in New Zealand, Australia, the United Kingdom and most of the United States.

The World Health Organization reports that in many instances national mental health legislation takes away the rights of persons with mental disorders rather than protecting rights, and is often outdated. In 1991, the United Nations adopted the Principles for the Protection of Persons with Mental Illness and the Improvement of Mental Health Care, which established minimum human rights standards of practice in the mental health field. In 2006, the UN formally agreed the Convention on the Rights of Persons with Disabilities to protect and enhance the rights and opportunities of disabled people, including those with psychosocial disabilities.

The term insanity, sometimes used colloquially as a synonym for mental illness, is often used technically as a legal term. The insanity defense may be used in a legal trial (known as the mental disorder defence in some countries).

The social stigma associated with mental disorders is a widespread problem. Some people believe those with serious mental illnesses cannot recover, or are to blame for problems. The US Surgeon General stated in 1999 that: "Powerful and pervasive, stigma prevents people from acknowledging their own mental health problems, much less disclosing them to others." Employment discrimination is reported to play a significant part in the high rate of unemployment among those with a diagnosis of mental illness. Efforts are being undertaken worldwide to eliminate the stigma of mental illness, although their methods and outcomes have sometimes been criticized.

A 2008 study by Baylor University researchers found that clergy in the US often deny or dismiss the existence of a mental illness. Of 293 Christian church members, more than 32 percent were told by their church pastor that they or their loved one did not really have a mental illness, and that the cause of their problem was solely spiritual in nature, such as a personal sin, lack of faith or demonic involvement. The researchers also found that women were more likely than men to get this response. All participants in both studies were previously diagnosed by a licensed mental health provider as having a serious mental illness. However, there is also research suggesting that people are often helped by extended families and supportive religious leaders who listen with kindness and respect, which can often contrast with usual practice in psychiatric diagnosis and medication.

Media coverage of mental illness comprises predominantly negative depictions, for example, of incompetence, violence or criminality, with far less coverage of positive issues such as accomplishments or human rights issues. Such negative depictions, including in children's cartoons, are thought to contribute to stigma and negative attitudes in the public and in those with mental health problems themselves, although more sensitive or serious cinematic portrayals have increased in prevalence.

In the United States, the Carter Center has created fellowships for journalists in South Africa, the U.S., and Romania, to enable reporters to research and write stories on mental health topics. Former US First Lady Rosalynn Carter began the fellowships not only to train reporters in how to sensitively and accurately discuss mental health and mental illness, but also to increase the number of stories on these topics in the news media. There is a World Mental Health Day, which the US and Canada subsume under a Mental Illness Awareness Week.

The general public have been found to hold a strong stereotype of dangerousness and desire for social distance from individuals described as mentally ill. A US national survey found that a higher percentage of people rate individuals described as displaying the characteristics of a mental disorder as "likely to do something violent to others", compared to the percentage of people who are rating individuals described as being "troubled".

Despite public or media opinion, national studies have indicated that severe mental illness does not independently predict future violent behavior, on average, and is not a leading cause of violence in society. There is a statistical association with various factors that do relate to violence (in anyone), such as substance abuse and various personal, social and economic factors.

In fact, findings consistently indicate that it is many times more likely that people diagnosed with a serious mental illness living in the community will be the victims rather than the perpetrators of violence. In a study of individuals diagnosed with "severe mental illness" living in a US inner-city area, a quarter were found to have been victims of at least one violent crime over the course of a year, a proportion eleven times higher than the inner-city average, and higher in every category of crime including violent assaults and theft. People with a diagnosis may find it more difficult to secure prosecutions, however, due in part to prejudice and being seen as less credible.

However, there are some specific diagnoses, such as childhood conduct disorder or adult antisocial personality disorder or psychopathy, which are defined by or inherently associated with conduct problems and violence. There are conflicting findings about the extent to which certain specific symptoms, notably some kinds of psychosis (hallucinations or delusions) that can occur in disorders such as schizophrenia, delusional disorder or mood disorder, are linked to an increased risk of serious violence on average. The mediating factors of violent acts, however, are most consistently found to be mainly socio-demographic and socio-economic factors such as being young, male, of lower socioeconomic status and, in particular, substance abuse (including alcoholism) to which some people may be particularly vulnerable.

High-profile cases have led to fears that serious crimes, such as homicide, have increased due to deinstitutionalization, but the evidence does not support this conclusion. Violence that does occur in relation to mental disorder (against the mentally ill or by the mentally ill) typically occurs in the context of complex social interactions, often in a family setting rather than between strangers. It is also an issue in health care settings and the wider community.

7

Trafficking in Persons and Smuggling of Migrants

It is important to distinguish between trafficking in persons and smuggling of migrants for two reasons:

— The constituent elements of the respective offences are different.

— The response required of your authorities will vary, depending on the offence. The definitions for trafficking in persons and migrant smuggling are found in the Protocol to Prevent, Suppress and Punish Trafficking in Persons, especially women and children (Trafficking Protocol) and the Protocol against the Smuggling of Migrants by Land, Sea and Air (Smuggling Protocol) respectively.

Trafficking in Persons

Article 3 of the Trafficking Protocol clarifies that trafficking in persons has three constituent elements:

— An act (what is done).

— The means (how it is done).

— Exploitative purpose (why it is done).

Article 5 further requires countries to ensure that the conduct contained in article 3 is criminalised in their domestic legislation. It is important to remember that the definition contained in the Trafficking Protocol is meant to provide a level of consistency and consensus around the world on the phenomenon of trafficking in persons; domestic legislation, however, need not follow the precise language of the Trafficking Protocol. Rather, domestic legislation should be adapted in accordance with domestic legal systems and give effect to the meaning and concepts contained in the Trafficking Protocol.

The Trafficking Protocol requires that the crime of trafficking be defined through a combination of the three constituent elements and not the individual components, though in some cases these individual elements will constitute criminal offences independently. For example, the act of abduction or the non-consensual application of force (assault) will likely constitute separate criminal offences under domestic criminal legislation. In criminal law terms, these three constituent elements can also be identified as the actus reus—the material or physical element(s)—and the men rea—the mental element. No conviction may be rendered in the absence of these two criminal law concepts, fundamental to criminal systems around the world.

Actus Reus Requirements

The actus reus or material elements of trafficking in persons vary depending on the legislation of your country. In the case of the crime of trafficking as defined in the Trafficking Protocol, the actus reus requirement is split into two parts.

1. The offence must include any one of the following:
   - — Recruiting.
   - — Transporting.
   - — Transferring.
   - — Harbouring.

— Receiving a person.

Some or all of these terms are likely to have a clearly defined meaning in your domestic legal system.

2. It must also contain at least one of the following means:
   — Use of force.
   — Threat of force.
   — Coercion.
   — Abduction.
   — Fraud.
   — Deception.
   — Abuse of power or of a position of vulnerability.
   — Giving or receiving of benefits.

Men Rea Requirement

The men rea requirement reflects the state of mind of the person charged with an offence. Only those with a sufficient "guilty mind" can be found liable for a criminal offence. In certain jurisdictions and in certain cases, criminal liability may be "strict" ("strict liability" offences).

The requisite mental element required in a trafficking in persons case is that the person committed the material act(s) with the intention that the victim be "exploited" (as defined by a country's domestic anti-trafficking legislation).

The Trafficking Protocol does not define exploitation but gives a non-exhaustive list of forms of exploitation:

> "shall include, at a minimum, the exploitation of the prostitution of others or other forms of sexual exploitation, forced labour or services, slavery, or practices similar to slavery, servitude or the removal of organs."

Again, it is important to remember that the Trafficking Protocol obligation to criminalise trafficking in persons does not require that domestic legislation use the precise language by the perpetrator when committing the material acts of the offence. It is the purpose that matters, not the practical result attained by the perpetrator. Thus, the fulfilment of the dolus specialist element does not require that the aim be actually achieved.

In other words, the "acts" and "means" of the perpetrator must aim to exploit the victim. It is not therefore necessary that the perpetrator actually exploits the victim contained in the definition of trafficking in persons. Rather, domestic legislation should be drafted in a way that is consistent with your domestic legal framework, provided it contains a combination of the constituent elements contained in the definition. An offence of trafficking in persons should not require that actual exploitation take place.

As is clear from the Trafficking Protocol, actual exploitation need not occur provided there is a manifestation of intention to exploit the individual. All that is required is that the accused committed one of the constituent acts, employing one of the listed means for the purpose or, put another way, with the intention that the individual be exploited. The mental element can be proven in a number of ways. It should be noted that the Trafficking Protocol requires that countries only criminalise trafficking in persons when conducted intentionally as per Article 5(1). This speaks to the mental element. However, countries are not precluded from allowing the men rea requirement to be established on a lesser standard, i.e. via recklessness, wilful blindness or even criminal negligence, subject to the requirements of the domestic legal system.

Other examples of trafficking in persons, as contemplated by the Trafficking Protocol Forced marriages may involve an act, means and purpose that fit the definition of trafficking as defined in the Protocol. The act may be transfer or receipt of a person; the means will include force, threats, coercion or abduction; the purpose may be sexual exploitation and/or servitude.

In some societies where a member of a family commits a crime, a young female from the offenders' family may be sent to live in servitude with a priest or with the victim's family to "repay" the crime. The act may be receipt or harbouring; the means may be coercion, abuse of power or of a position of vulnerability; the purpose may be sexual or labour exploitation, servitude or slavery.

Diplomatic staff frequently employ servants. In a number of cases around the world some of these servants have been recruited and forced to provide labour within the households. Forcible abduction and conscription of children and adults into armed forces during times of conflict can also be prosecuted as a trafficking crime. Children are especially vulnerable to military recruitment due to their emotional and physical immaturity. The act may be recruitment, transporting, or receiving a child or adult, the means (in the case of adults) may be the use or threat of use of force, or the abuse of a position of vulnerability and the purpose may be servitude, forced labour, or sexual exploitation.

In some countries, particularly those with an already established adoption market, illicit adoption practices are becoming more common and can be prosecuted under the umbrella of trafficking crimes. Children may be forcibly separated from their mothers who were coerced into signing blank documents that were later made into illegal contracts. The act may be transporting or receiving a child and the purpose may be slavery or sexual exploitation. It is unnecessary to establish a means when the trafficking victim is under 18 years of age, however coercion, fraud and deception are commonly used on the mother to provide signatures, blood samples and birth certificates.

Peacekeeping and post-conflict operations create circumstances in which trafficking in persons, mainly women for sexual exploitation, has flourished in the past. The act may be recruiting, transferring or receiving, the means may be coercion, deception or abuse of power or of a position of vulnerability and the purpose may be sexual exploitation, servitude, or forced labour.

The Issue of Consent

Article 3(b) of the Trafficking Protocol states that the consent of a victim of trafficking in persons to the intended exploitation is irrelevant once it is demonstrated that deception, coercion, force or other prohibited means have been used. Consent, therefore, cannot be used as a defence to absolve a person from criminal responsibility. In trafficking cases involving children, the Trafficking Protocol states that trafficking in persons is made out regardless of the use of prohibited means.

Both of these instances reflect the simple fact that no person can consent to being exploited, because in the case of adults, consent has been negated through the use of improper means and, in the case of children, their vulnerable position makes it impossible for them to provide consent in the first place. The issue of consent is complex since consent can take many forms. The following examples illustrate the question of consent.

Example of Negated Consent

Twenty-three-year-old Anita lives in Central Asia. She wants to live and work abroad and one day answers a newspaper advertisement for waitressing work abroad that specifically requires the ability to speak her native language. Anna answers the ad and when her plane lands, a man takes her to an apartment where she meets a dozen other women.

She asks them if they all work at the restaurant as waitresses. They laugh at her and one says:

> "Restaurant? You're not going to work at a restaurant! You'll find out tonight where you are working!" Anna is held for six months and prostituted by her traffickers, who claim to have purchased her for several hundred dollars. They say she owes them money for her plane ticket, accommodation and food. They beat her when she refuses a client.

Example of Deceit Regarding the Conditions of Work

Bela lives in a South American country and works as a prostitute. One day, a regular client who visits her periodically when conducting business in her city, tells her that she could make much more money in the North American city where he lives. This client, called Nick, tells her that the prostitutes in his city go out to the clubs all the time, make a lot of money, and have a lot of fun. Nick tells her he will buy her plane ticket, so Bela agrees and gets a visa to travel to the new city.

Nick meets Bela at the airport and she stays at his house for a few days. One day, a group of men come to the house to take her to her new place of work. The men give Nick $US 10,000 and take Bela to a town outside the city. There she is put to work in three brothels and has to have sex with up to nine customers a day. If she refuses, her debt is increased. All of the money paid for her services goes either to the brothel owners or to the men who bought her. She is told that she cannot leave before her debt is reimbursed. She sees violence used against some of her friends.

Migrant Smuggling

Article 3 of the Smuggling Protocol establishes that migrant smuggling is comprised of the following elements:

— Procuring the illegal entry of another person.

— Into another state.

— For the purpose of financial or material gain.

Article 3(b) further defines "illegal entry" as the crossing of (international) borders without complying with the necessary requirements for legal entry into the receiving State. Article 6 of the Smuggling Protocol requires, amongst other things, the criminalisation of the offence of migrant smuggling.

Examples of Criminal Legislation

Belgium

Article 77 of the Immigration Law criminalises smuggling in persons, and article ibis penalises involvement in the entry into Belgium of a foreigner if violence, intimidation, coercion or deception were used, or abusing the vulnerability of a foreigner in terms of his or her illegal status, precarious situation, pregnancy, disease or disability. Both laws are used to prosecute smuggling in persons, with the difference that violations of Ibis carry a harsher sentence. Aggravating circumstances include violations conducted on a "regular" basis or carried out by an organised association (consisting of two or more persons) and the penalties increase to 10 to 15 years and a fine.

Colombia

Colombia's broad trafficking law includes smuggling offences and states that "anyone who promotes, induces, constrains, enables, finances, cooperates or participates in a person's transfer within the national territory or abroad by resorting to any form of violence, ruse or deception, for exploitation purposes, to lead such person to work in prostitution, pornography, debt bondage, begging, forced labour, servile marriage, slavery for purposes of obtaining financial profit or any other benefit either for himself or for another person, shall incur 10 to 15 years' imprisonment and a fine..." The law criminalises facilitation of illegal migration for the purpose of profit and has provisions regarding obtaining profit or property from smuggling punishable by six to eight years' imprisonment.

Elements of a Case of Migrant Smuggling

The actus reus or material elements of migrant smuggling vary depending on the legislation of your country. In the case of the crime of smuggling, as defined in the Smuggling Protocol, the actus reus requirement includes the following:

— Procurement of an illegal entry of another person.

— Entry into another country by the other person, a smuggled migrant who is neither a national nor permanent resident of that country.

— Agreement to receive a financial or other material benefit.

The Smuggling Protocol does not define "procurement". Generally speaking, this refers to the act of bringing about a specific thing; in the case of migrant smuggling, the illegal entry of another person into a country.

The men rea requirement reflects the state of mind of the person charged with an offence. Only those with a sufficient "guilty mind" can be found liable for a criminal offence. In certain jurisdictions and in certain cases, criminal liability may be imposed in "strict liability" offences even in the absence of men rea.

The requisite mental element required in a smuggling of migrants case is that the person committed the material act(s) intentionally and in order to obtain a financial or other material benefit, directly or indirectly. Hence, smuggling for non-profit purposes does not fall under the scope of the Smuggling Protocol.

The mental element can be proven in a number of ways. It should be noted that the Smuggling Protocol requires that countries only criminalise smuggling of migrants when conducted intentionally as per article 6(1). This speaks to the mental element. However, countries are not precluded from allowing the men rea requirement to be established on a lesser standard, i.e. via recklessness, wilful blindness or even criminal negligence, subject to the requirements of the domestic legal system.

Again, it is important to remember that the Smuggling Protocol obligation to criminalise smuggling of migrants does not require that domestic legislation use the precise language contained in the definition of smuggling of migrants. Rather, domestic legislation should be drafted in a way that is consistent with your domestic legal framework, provided it contains a combination of the constituent elements contained in the definition. It is also important to note that migrants are not to be made liable to criminal prosecution under the Smuggling Protocol for the fact of having been the object of smuggling as per article 6 of the Smuggling Protocol.

Differences between Trafficking in Persons and Migrant Smuggling

In practice, it may be difficult to distinguish between these two crimes in the first instance. In many cases, victims of trafficking may first start out as smuggled migrants. Consequently, in investigating trafficking in persons cases, it may sometimes be necessary to rely on measures against smuggling. It is critical, however, that those investigating smuggling cases be familiar with the crime of trafficking in persons as the consequences of treating a trafficking case as one of migrant smuggling can be severe for the victim.

Identifying the Differences

In some cases it may be difficult to quickly ascertain whether a case is one of human smuggling or trafficking. The distinctions between smuggling and trafficking are often very subtle and there are overlaps. Identifying whether a case is one of trafficking in persons or people smuggling can be very difficult for a number of reasons:

- Some trafficked persons might start their journey by agreeing to be smuggled into a country illegally, but find themselves deceived, coerced or forced into an exploitative situation later in the process.
- Traffickers may present an opportunity that sounds more like smuggling to potential victims. They could be asked to pay a fee in common with other people who are smuggled. However, the intention of the trafficker from the outset is the exploitation of the victim. The fee was part of the fraud and deception and a way to make a bit more money.
- Smuggling may be the planned intention at the outset but a too-good-to-miss opportunity to traffic people presents itself to the smugglers/traffickers at some point in the process.
- Criminals may both smuggle and traffic people, employing the same routes.
- Conditions for a smuggled person along the journey may be so bad it is difficult to believe a person could have consented to this.

Having said this, there are a number of key differences between migrant smuggling and trafficking in persons:

Consent

Migrant smuggling generally involves the consent of those being smuggled. Victims of trafficking, on the other hand, have either never consented or, if they initially consented, that consent has been rendered meaningless by the improper means of the traffickers.

Trans-nationality

To smuggle a person means to facilitate the person's illegal border crossing and entry into another country. Trafficking in persons, on the other hand, need not involve the crossing of any border. Where it does, the legality or illegality of the border crossing is irrelevant. Thus, while migrant smuggling is always, by definition, trans-national, trafficking in persons need not be.

Exploitation

The relationship between smuggler and smuggled migrant usually ends after the facilitation of the border crossing. Smuggling fees are paid up front or upon arrival. The smuggler has no intention to exploit the smuggled person after arrival. Smuggler and migrant are partners, albeit disparate, in a commercial operation that the migrant enters willingly. Trafficking involves the ongoing exploitation of the victims in some manner to generate illicit profits for the traffickers. It is the intention of the trafficker that the relationship with the exploited victims will be a continuous one and extend beyond the crossing of the border in the final destination. Smuggling can become trafficking, e.g. when the smuggler sells the person and the accumulated debt, or deceives/coerces/forces the person to work off transportation costs under exploitative conditions.

Source of the Profit

One important indicator of whether a case is one of smuggling or of trafficking in persons is how the offenders generate their income. Smugglers generate their income from fees to move people. The trafficker in contrast continues to exert control over the trafficked victim in order to achieve additional profits through the ongoing exploitation of the victim.

Appropriate Charges

As explained above, the offence of trafficking in persons may involve many different acts and many different actors. The offence is committed by acts of recruitment, transportation, transfer, harbouring or receipt of persons, by means of the threat or use of force or other forms of coercion, of abduction, of fraud, of deception, of the abuse of power or of a position of vulnerability or of the giving or receiving of payments or benefits to achieve the consent of a person having control over another person, for the purpose of exploitation.

Trafficking cases, by their nature, are very likely to involve other offences. These offences may be an integral part of the trafficking process, and can be used to prove that an element of the trafficking in persons offence has been committed. They can also be charged separately or utilised as alternative charges, depending on the legal system. They can also be called underlying offences to trafficking.

Other offences may be committed against the trafficking victim or others, but would not be an integral part of the trafficking offence. These should be charged separately.

Examples

Identifying whether trafficking in persons or smuggling of migrants has taken place can be difficult in practice. Please look at these examples which illustrate the basic differences between the two. Please note that cases have to be seen in the context of domestic law and local circumstances. In this module we examine cases in light of the Trafficking in Persons and Smuggling of Migrants Protocol.

Appropriate Charges

As explained above, the offence of trafficking in persons may involve many different acts and many different actors. The offence is committed by acts of recruitment, transportation, transfer, harbouring or receipt of persons, by means of the threat or use of force or other forms of coercion, of abduction, of fraud, of deception, of the abuse of power or of a position of vulnerability or of the giving or receiving of payments or benefits to achieve the consent of a person having control over another person, for the purpose of exploitation.

Trafficking cases, by their nature, are very likely to involve other offences. These offences may be an integral part of the trafficking process, and can be used to prove that an element of the trafficking in persons offence has been committed. They can also be charged separately or utilised as alternative charges, depending on the legal system. They can also be called underlying offences to trafficking.

Other offences may be committed against the trafficking victim or others, but would not be an integral part of the trafficking offence. These should be charged separately. Underlying offences to trafficking may include but are not limited to:

— Slavery.

— Slavery-like practices.

— Servitude.

— Forced or compulsory labour.

— Debt bondage.

— Forced marriage.

— Forced abortion.

— Extortion.

— Torture.

— Cruel, inhumane or degrading treatment.
— Rape.
— Sexual assault.
— Assault.
— Bodily injury.
— Murder.
— Kidnapping.
— Abduction.
— Unlawful confinement.
— Labour exploitation.
— Withholding identity papers.
— Violations of immigration law.
— Money-laundering.
— Corruption.
— Abuse of office.
— Smuggling of migrants.

Investigation and prosecution of the individual acts mentioned above can be particularly useful in situations and in countries where:

— A distinct criminal offence of trafficking does not yet exist.
— The penalties for trafficking do not sufficiently reflect the nature of the crime and do not have any deterrent effects.

In cases where the existing evidence is not sufficient in order to prosecute for trafficking but may be sufficient to prosecute for such underlying offences. In systems that allow plea bargains, in general it would be recommended to charge for all possible offences, so that in the case of a plea bargain, some charges may be crossed out. Where the evidence is there, for a number of reasons, you should aim at prosecuting perpetrators under the offence of trafficking in persons. If possible in your legal system, utilise underlying offences as alternative charges to increase chances for a conviction.

If the criminal offence of trafficking exists in your jurisdiction, the underlying offences are particularly useful in situations where you do not find sufficient evidence for the prosecution of trafficking. The evidence may still be sufficient for prosecution of the individual criminal acts, the underlying offences to trafficking such as unlawful confinement, sexual assault, bodily injury, withholding of identity documents, etc. In these situations your only option may be to prosecute for the individual criminal acts.

Even if you initially choose to prosecute traffickers under the offence of trafficking in persons but the evidence does not support your case beyond reasonable doubt, the evidence may suffice for conviction for the underlying offences. Hence, the underlying offences can also be invoked in addition to prosecuting under the offence of trafficking in persons. The provisions can also be invoked as additional or overlapping offences to demonstrate the seriousness of a particular trafficking operation.

As a practitioner you know that investigating suspects and prosecuting defendants with trafficking offences can be very complex, time consuming and costly. It is therefore not surprising that there are a number of examples of cases where trafficking in persons is present, indeed is the driving force—may be the reason deter of a case—but the only charges laid are for the underlying offences such as unlawful confinement, sexual assault, bodily injury, withholding of identity documents, etc.

Failing to prosecute for trafficking offences may be appealing in the short term, but has a number of potentially significant long term consequences. In many occasions a trafficking charge may give a victim access to victim support services, protection, and assistance that would not otherwise be available. These victim support services can include the possibility of a reflection period, temporary or even permanent residence status in the destination country, and support services at various levels, including accommodation, health care, legal and psychological counselling and access to resettlement packages. This is of importance to you for a number of reasons.

Trauma can affect the quality of the testimony of trafficking victims. Providing support, protection and assistance to victims of trafficking helps the victim overcome the most severe consequences of trauma and helps you to build the trust of a trafficking victim. You are not likely to get that trust if you cannot provide proper support for victims. Without trust you are unlikely to get the quality of testimony you require.

In many jurisdictions the laying of a charge for trafficking in persons will trigger various protection and assistance measures for victims. It may also mean that the victim is not prosecuted for offences he or she may have committed in the process of trafficking. Prosecuting the victim for offences he or she may have committed as a direct consequence of being trafficking may destroy the relationship that you have to build in order to gain the best possible witness testimony for your case. It may directly significantly weaken the witness testimony and contribute to the victim's decision not to cooperate with the criminal justice system. Failing to prosecute for trafficking in persons offences may also mean that the wider trafficking networks are left to operate without any disruptions.

Jurisdiction

Trafficking in persons cases may involve a number of jurisdictions. Where this is the case a decision has to be taken about which jurisdiction the prosecution should take place in. There are a number of principles that should guide this decision. It is very important to identify as soon as you can that it is possible a case can be prosecuted in more than one jurisdiction.

Once this possibility is identified the next consideration is where it is most feasible to prosecute. Any decision made on which jurisdiction is best placed to prosecute should be made on a case-by-case basis taking into account all the relevant factors. The basic principle underlying any decision is that a person should not be prosecuted more than once for the same criminal conduct. This applies even where a person has been acquitted of a charge relating to that conduct in another jurisdiction. This is known as the principle of in idem or double jeopardy.

Prosecutions should take place in the jurisdiction where the majority of criminalist took place or where the majority of the loss took place. In trafficking cases, this is often, but not automatically, the destination location where exploitation took place.

8

Global Menace of HIV/AIDS

HIV kills by weakening the body's immune system until it can no longer fight infection. Opportunistic infections are illnesses such as pneumonia, meningitis, some cancers, tuberculosis (TB), or other parasitic, viral, and fungal infections that occur when the immune system is weakened.

HIV generally progresses over a decade before developing into AIDS, but there is a long delay after infection before symptoms become evident. Early HIV-related symptoms include chronic fatigue, diarrhoea, fever, weight loss, persistent cough, skin rashes, herpes and other oral infections, swelling of the lymph nodes, and memory loss or other mental changes. AIDS is almost always fatal without treatment, although a few individuals have survived with AIDS untreated for up to 20 years. Current drug regimen, such as highly active nitrate rivalry therapy (HAART), slow the virus' replication in the body. Slower replication rates lessen the burden on the immune system, thereby reducing HIV-related illnesses and allowing patients to live longer, higher-quality lives. There is no cure for AIDS: The disease resurrects if HAART is halted.

Risk and Vulnerability

When AIDS was first identified in the 1980s, public health

officials assumed its spread could be halted by informing people how to protect themselves from infection and by safeguarding blood supplies. This approach has been successful in politically organised communities with access to information and resources:

It reduced incidence among white gay men in North America, Australia, and Western Europe, for example. But population in less developed and socially fragmented countries had little access to accurate information or effective prevention programs, and the virus continued to spread. In the late 1980s, as the epidemic surged and shifted from people with high-risk behaviour to the general population, especially in developing countries, public health professionals realised they needed to better understand the causes of individual infection and the forces driving the pandemic.

They knew HIV transmission was linked to specific behaviour such as having multiple sex partners, commercial sex, and injecting drug use, but they also realised that these behaviours were influenced by political, economic, social, cultural, and environmental factors—including poverty, military conflict, powerlessness, and gender inequality. Understanding the factors High-Risk Behaviour High-risk behaviour—unprotected sex with multiple partners, injecting drug use, and commercial sex—can increase vulnerability to HIV infection. While heterosexual sex between multiple partners has been the driving force behind the epidemics in sub-Saharan Africa, injecting drug use and commercial sex have been the main drivers of epidemics in Asia.

Injecting drug users are more susceptible to HIV infection because they sometimes use contaminated needles and syringes, which are an efficient mode of transmission. Sex workers face increased risk of infection because they engage in sex with multiple partners, often with no protection. The interaction between commercial sex and injecting drug use heightens vulnerability, as many injecting drug users engage in commercial sex to finance their drug habits and a considerable proportion of sex workers also inject drugs.

Many countries have seen high levels of HIV for injecting drug users and sex workers, but they have yet to experience epidemics within the general population. However, once HIV is established in high-risk groups, it can easily spread to the general public via bridge groups, such as clients of sex workers. These bridge population can infect their own spouses and partners with HIV. Risk and Vulnerability of Women Whereas men were most affected at the beginning of the epidemic, women's rates of new infection now surpass men's, especially in countries where women live in poverty and have relatively low status. In sub-Saharan Africa, women make up 57 percent of adults living with HIV. The gender gap is especially pronounced among Africans younger than age 25.

In sub-Saharan Africa, women ages 15 to 24 are three times more likely to be infected than young men their age. Biological, cultural, and socioeconomic conditions contribute to women's greater vulnerability to HIV. During unprotected vaginal intercourse, a woman's risk of becoming infected is up to four times higher than that of a man. The vagina has a greater area of susceptible tissue compared with the male urethra and often sustains microcornea during intercourse. In addition, HIV-infected semen typically contains a higher viral concentration than do vaginal secretions.

The risk of HIV infection increases for people who have other sexually transmitted infections (STIs). Research shows that some untreated STIs in either partner can increase the risk of HIV transmission as much as tenfold. This is especially significant for women because many STI cases in women go untreated. Women's symptoms are often latent or difficult to see, and many women who have been diagnosed with STIs do not receive medical treatment.

Socioeconomic factors, including women's lack of access to education or personal income, and unequal property rights perpetuate women's greater vulnerability to HIV infection. Many women fear their husbands or partners will abandon them if they try to control how and when they have sex and whether their partner uses a condom. Moreover, poverty drives some women into the sex industry, where sexual trafficking and commercial sex promote continued exposure to HIV. Furthermore, men control the main tool for reducing the risk of sexual transmission of HIV:

> the male condom. Even though the female condom has improved prevention options for women, men's involvement is still crucial. Cultural traditions such as male dominance and older men's preference for young women contribute to women's vulnerability. Throughout the world, prevailing views about masculinity encourage men to undertake risky sexual behaviours—multiple sex partners, alcohol consumption prior to intercourse, and sexual violence—that make women more vulnerable to HIV and other STIs.

In many cases, a wife's marriage and fidelity do not protect her from HIV because her husband's sexual behaviour before or during marriage puts her at risk. For example, in India, many new infections occur among married women whose husbands have frequented sex workers and, according to one study, married women in Nicaragua are twice as likely to be HIV-positive as are sex workers. Violence against women, including sexual violence, is most often inflicted by a husband or partner and can also be a factor in HIV infection.

According to one South African study, women who experienced violence from their partners were 48 percent more likely to be HIV-positive than those who had not. Young girls are at even greater risk of infection because of their social vulnerability both before and during marriage. Most infections in young women are a result of unprotected sex and reflect a power imbalance that limits women's ability to negotiate or control sexual interactions, especially with older men. Additionally, young girls face heightened biological risks because their reproductive tracts are not yet fully developed.

High-Risk Situations

Military conflicts and natural disasters bring together populations with different levels of HIV infection, thereby increasing the potential for new infections. During such times, socioeconomic and health structures begin to break down as populations are displaced from their homes and communities. The massive population dislocations during the 1994 genocide in Rwanda, for example, mixed urban populations with high levels of HIV with rural populations with low levels of HIV, helping expand the epidemic into rural areas. In recent years, more than 50 million people in over 70 countries have been affected by emergencies stemming from armed conflict and natural disasters. While all population groups in emergency situations may face increased risks of HIV, women and children are the most vulnerable and least able to protect themselves.

Some engage in risky behaviours, such as sex work, in an effort to survive. Children may be separated from their parents, recruited as child soldiers, or placed in situations that may make them more vulnerable to infection. Additionally, as security situations deteriorate, women and girls are often subjected to sexual violence and rape. Military personnel also face heightened risks of contracting or spreading HIV through risky sex during long deployment away from home.

Given the immediate needs of health care, shelter, food, and water, the threat of HIV infection has not historically been a priority in emergency situations. But humanitarian and relief efforts are now beginning to integrate HIV programs into emergency responses. In some cases, especially when conflicts limit the freedom of movement, the greatest threat of HIV transmission can occur during the period of peace following a time of conflict. For example, the civil war in Angola probably slowed the spread of HIV because trade and travel were halted for almost three decades. However, the threat of HIV in Angola has risen since the end of the war in 2002 because of the return of refugees, the opening of borders, increased trade, and more travel.

Labour migration—which involves millions of people every year—also leads to increased vulnerability and spread of HIV. Some of the factors that contribute to migrant and mobile workers' increased vulnerability include frequent travel, long separations from spouses or partners, limited access to health services, and minimal social contact or recreational opportunities. Without family and community support systems, migrants are more likely to engage in risky behaviours and potentially pass those risks on to their own family and community members.

Orphans and Vulnerable Children

The rising HIV infection rates among women, particularly in sub-Saharan Africa, expose children to increased HIV risk even before they are born. In 16 sub-Saharan African countries, at least 5 percent of pregnant women ages 15 to 24 attending prenatal clinics between 2001 and 2003 were HIV-positive. However, fewer than 10 percent of pregnant women were offered services to prevent mother-to-child transmission. In the absence of preventive measures, approximately one-third of children born to HIV-positive mothers will contract HIV. UN AIDS estimates that 2.3 million children were living with HIV at the end of 2005.

Fewer than 5 percent of children who need podiatric AIDS treatment are receiving it. Many HIV-infected children bear a double impact: Not only are they living with the disease themselves, but they have also lost one or both parents to AIDS. At the end of 2003, 15 million children had lost at least one parent to AIDS.

The number of children orphaned by AIDS is increasing at an unprecedented rate. Without AIDS, the percentage of children who are orphans would be expected to decline because of general improvements in health, but AIDS is dramatically increasing the percentage and number of orphans, especially in countries hard hit by the epidemic. As more parents develop AIDS and die, the number of orphans will continue to rise over the next 10 years. In sub-Saharan Africa, AIDS had orphaned 12 million children by 2003; by 2010, 18 million children are expected to be orphaned by AIDS. In South Africa alone, the number of orphans is expected to increase from 2.2 million in 2003 to 3.1 million in 2010.

Children in resource-poor environments are exceedingly vulnerable to a variety of adverse conditions even before the AIDS-related death of a parent or guardian. Basic needs like schooling, food, shelter, and health care are jeopardised, while children face an increased risk of abuse, exploitation, and social isolation. Psychosocial needs are significant as children deal with the trauma of impending or actual parental loss as well as possible disclosure issues about their parent's or their own HIV status, adjustment to new living and family circumstances, and real or perceived increases in economic and family responsibilities.

Children may serve as the primary caretaker of ailing parents, assume responsibility for younger siblings, or assume additional duties in the household. If the primary wage earner falls ill, children may leave school to find work to help support the family. Illnesses in the family may also divert funds that were previously available for school fees. Families of people living with HIV and AIDS often encounter stigma and discrimination that may deny children access to education and even health care.

Children orphaned by AIDS are at an increased risk of exploitation and abuse. Weak or poorly enforced laws can result in orphans being cheated out of their inheritance. Economic demands may force children, girls in particular, into commercial sex work or relationships with older men to obtain food, shelter, or money. Without the protection of a parent or loving guardian, children may become victims of trafficking, exploitive labour conditions, or violence. These risky conditions increase the orphaned child's vulnerability to HIV.

Health and Demographic Effects

AIDS has exacted a devastating toll on population and health over the last 25 years. The number of people living with HIV has surged from a few thousand in the 1980s to 40 million by 2005, and has spread to all world regions. The epidemic has triggered an upsurge in previously rare infections and malignancies and is contributing to an explosive TB epidemic around the world. HIV has reversed hard-won gains in child survival and life expectancy in sub-Saharan Africa and in a growing number of countries and communities worldwide. Because AIDS tends to strike the young and sexually active, AIDS deaths have also distorted the age and sex profiles of the populations in heavily affected communities and countries. The unbalanced ratios affect population growth as well as the social and economic health of these areas.

HIV and Tuberculosis

Tuberculosis is re-emerging in many parts of the world and

now infects about one-third of the world's population. Some countries now face HIV and TB epidemics simultaneously. In sub-Saharan Africa, up to 70 percent of TB patients are infected with HIV. AIDS and TB interact destructively, each hastening the progression of the other. TB is a leading cause of death among people with HIV and is responsible for an estimated 13 percent of AIDS deaths. Most people infected with TB, but not HIV, remain healthy: Only 5 percent to 10 percent will develop an active case of TB. HIV, however, triggers the active––and thus infectious—form of TB. A person with an active case of pulmonary TB can infect an average of 10 to 15 people every year with TB if he or she does not receive treatment.

HIV infection also makes TB more difficult to diagnose. People with HIV or AIDS often develop multi-drug-resistant TB, detectable only through special laboratory tests often not available in low-income countries. TB is curable in HIV-infected individuals, but treatment is much more expensive and typically requires a strict regimen of drugs for approximately six months. Strict adherence to treatment often is difficult for residents in developing countries, where access to health care is limited.

HIV and Malaria

Malaria and HIV are the most common infections and the most important causes of death and illness in sub-Saharan Africa. An estimated 30 million Africans are infected with HIV, and between 300 million and 500 million people suffer from malaria each year. There is increasing evidence that malaria and HIV interact such that HIV infection reduces the effectiveness of antimalarial drugs. HIV is associated with increased risk of malaria infection; more severe disease and death; and in pregnant women, more episodes of malaria and fever, and more adverse birth outcomes.

Lower Life Expectancy

AIDS is the fourth leading cause of death worldwide. In 2005, UN AIDS estimated that 3.1 million adults and children died of AIDS, of whom 2.4 million were in sub-Saharan Africa. Conversely, AIDS-associated deaths in some countries have decreased dramatically, because of effective new medications. In Brazil, government policies to provide universal treatment of AIDS patients reduced AIDS deaths as much as 70 percent between 1996 and 2002 one-third of children infected with HIV through mother-to-child transmission die before they reach age 1, and approximately 60 percent die by age 5.

The UN estimated that child mortality increased in South Africa from 62 to 74 deaths per 1,000 children under age 5 between the late 1990s and early 2000s. If not for AIDS mortality, under mortality would have been 43 deaths per 1,000 children. During the same period in Swaziland, under mortality rose from 109 to 143 deaths per 1,000 children; it would have been 73 in 2003 without the AIDS epidemic.

Improvements in public health and living standards throughout the world boosted average life expectancy in the mid- to late 1980s, but the surge of AIDS deaths has halted progress in many countries and caused a precipitous decline in several countries in sub-Saharan Africa. Lesotho's life expectancy is projected at 39 years in 2015–2020, but would have risen to 69 years without the AIDS epidemic. Some countries outside of sub-Saharan Africa are also experiencing AIDS-related reductions in life expectancy.

AIDS shortened projected life expectancy for 2015–2020 by four years in Cambodia and by seven years in Haiti. In sub-Saharan Africa, where women are infected with HIV at younger ages and in larger numbers than men, some countries are seeing even lower life expectancies among women. Between 2000 and 2005, female life expectancy dropped below male life expectancy because of AIDS in Kenya, Malawi, Zambia, and Zimbabwe. Kenya posted the largest difference—46 years for women and 48 years for men. Slower Population Growth Populations continue to grow in many heavily affected countries, although the growth is less than it would be in the absence of AIDS.

In Uganda, for example, the UN projects the population at 51 million by 2020, up from 29 million in 2005. If the country had not experienced an AIDS epidemic, the 2020 total would be about 5 million higher. The effect is much greater in South Africa, where AIDS mortality will nearly halt population growth in the next 15 years despite high fertility. South Africa is projected to add fewer than 1 million people to its 2005 population of 47.4 million in 15 years. If the country had escaped the AIDS epidemic, the UN estimates South Africa's 2020 population would be 63.1 million.

AIDS-related deaths are altering the age structure in severely affected countries. In southern Africa between 1985 and 1990, most deaths occurred among children under age 5 and adults over age 60, while only one-fifth of all deaths were among adults ages 20 to 49. Between 2000 and 2005, high AIDS mortality among young and middle-age adults meant that people ages 20 to 49 accounted for almost 60 percent of all deaths. South Africa embodies many of the changes projected for populations severely affected by AIDS. By 2020, fewer children will be born because of deaths and lower fertility among HIV-positive women. Many children will die of AIDS-related causes during childhood.

Social and Economic Impact

In heavily affected countries, HIV has overwhelmed public health systems and has stretched health care providers, infrastructure, and budgets beyond capacity. However, AIDS is much more than a health crisis. Its effects extend to nearly every dimension of social and economic life, especially in the worst-affected countries. Although the magnitude of the epidemic varies, in every country, AIDS primarily strikes adults between ages 25 and 45—people who were infected in their adolescent and young adult years. HIV and AIDS rob employees from the labour force, providers and caretakers from families, and teachers from communities. Public Health Burden Health sectors feel the impact of HIV through such direct costs as the expense of medical treatment, supplies, and personnel, and through such indirect costs as falling numbers of trained medical providers and increasing stress on health systems struggling to respond to the epidemic.

Global Challenges

HIV and AIDS continue to overwhelm the health systems in many countries. People living with HIV generally have a range of health care needs, spanning primary care and basic treatment for infections to hospitalisation and psychosocial counselling. Where antiretroviral drugs are available, health systems need to monitor patients and manage the complex treatment regimens.

The increased need for care is especially problematic in countries that already find it hard to meet the most basic health care needs of their populations. WHO has reported that nations need between US$35 and US$40 per capita each year to finance minimum general health services packages, including antiretroviral therapy for people living with AIDS. However, the average amount spent in 2001 was US$23, and only US$6 of this came from public spending.

Many countries, including some of the poorest, are increasing their domestic spending on HIV and AIDS. South Africa increased HIV/AIDS spending in its 2003/2004 national budget by 86 percent from the previous fiscal year. AIDS is usurping health sector resources needed to treat other health problems. In many hospitals in sub-Saharan Africa, for example, AIDS patients are crowding out other patients:

> AIDS patients frequently occupy more than half of hospital beds in some sub-Saharan Africa countries. In Cote devoir and Uganda, between 50 percent and 80 percent of adult hospital beds are occupied by patients with HIV-related conditions. The loss of health care staff to AIDS is another blow to the health care sector in heavily affected countries. Their loss is particularly painful given the escalating need for their professional skills as more people fall ill with AIDS. According to the health service in South Africa, 14 percent of staff (mostly nurses) died from AIDS between 1997 and 2001. AIDS also undermines health workers' morale as their workload and stress increase and they witness high mortality among children, young adults, and colleagues.

Impacts on Business, Agriculture, and Labour

Because AIDS affects people in their prime working ages, businesses are suffering severe effects from the epidemic. This is especially true in some sub-Saharan African countries, where as much as one-third of the work-engage population is infected with HIV. In high-prevalence countries, AIDS is consuming business profits because of three primary factors: increased operating costs, decreased productivity, and declining markets.

AIDS was initially believed to be primarily an urban phenomenon, but it now clearly threatens the lives and livelihoods of rural communities throughout the less developed world. AIDS-related deaths among farm workers threaten agricultural production and food security, most notably in sub-Saharan Africa where a large segment of society relies on agriculture. The Food and Agriculture Organisation (FAO) estimates that 7 million agricultural workers died of AIDS between 1985 and 2000 in the 25 hardest-hit countries in sub-Saharan Africa. FAO projects that 16 million more agricultural workers could die because of AIDS by 2020. In the worst-affected countries, losses in the agricultural labour force will range from 13 percent in Tanzania to 26 percent in Namibia by 2020. The loss of agricultural labourers in southern Africa will cause an estimated 3 percent loss in grain output. By disrupting agricultural production, AIDS can undermine countries' export capacity and thus their ability to earn foreign exchange. In Africa, agriculture accounts for 70 percent of employment, 24 percent of the gross domestic product, and 40 percent of the foreign exchange earnings. The International Labour Organisation (ILO) reports that subsistence agriculture employs 80 percent of the population of Swaziland, and export farming is responsible for 10 percent of the gross domestic product.

Farm households coping with AIDS may sell assets such as livestock, equipment, or land to support ill family members and pay for funeral expenses. Time devoted to care, funerals, and mourning of family members with AIDS reduces productivity and jeopardises households' ability to produce and purchase food. Moreover, important knowledge and skills are lost as deaths mount among the agricultural population. Women in agricultural households are particularly hard hit since they often provide the labour for farming, but must increasingly spend their time caring for sick family members.

Without the necessary labour and resources for planting and harvesting, some families leave their land. A survey in Zambia showed that chronically ill heads of households in rural areas reduced the area of land they cultivated by more than half, reducing crop production and food availability.

As incomes decline and more money is spent on health care, less money is available to spend on food, which can lead to malnutrition. Nutritional deficiencies can speed up the progression from HIV to AIDS and increase susceptibility to opportunistic infections. People living with AIDS need more calories than other people, especially if they have suffered significant weight loss. Individuals on antiretroviral drugs also have specific nutritional needs, and inadequate nutrition can affect their tolerance to the drugs and adherence to drug regimens.

Imapcts on Governance and Public Service

In countries heavily affected by HIV, the epidemic affects governance and public service in three main ways: The country loses hard-to-replace political leaders and civil servants; revenues decline and costs rise; and demand for social services increases. Taken together, these factors exert significant pressure on the governments of less developed countries.

At the highest levels, AIDS is taking the lives of national leaders—including ministers, parliamentarians, and cabinet members—although most of these are not classified as AIDS deaths because the families fear stigmatisation. Nations are losing their leaders and their years of political experience, undermining future national stability and security. Zambia held 14 special elections between 1964 and 1984 because of the death of an incumbent. From 1985, when the first case of HIV was recorded in the country, to 2003, Zambia held 59 by-elections due to incumbent deaths, of which occurred when the epidemic was in full force. The ranks of civil servants are also being depleted, Deaths among skilled civil servants are especially difficult to absorb in countries with low levels of literacy and education.

Many of these countries rely on a small pool of staff members to develop and administer services. Declining revenues and rising costs compound the loss of civil servants. In heavily affected countries, AIDS is reducing productivity and earnings. In 33 countries in sub-Saharan

Africa, the annual growth rate for the gross domestic product per capita declined by 0.7 percent between 1992 and 2002 because of the AIDS epidemic. Meanwhile, domestic government spending on AIDS has increased considerably. Between 1999 and 2002, low- and middle-income countries doubled their expenditures on AIDS programs to US$995 million. At the same time that costs rise and revenues decline, the demands on public services increase.

HIV generally affects the poorest households disproportionately, contributing to rising poverty and greater social welfare needs. Furthermore, millions of orphaned children will require new or expanded public services. Funding or investments in some public services are reduced because of increased expenditures on health care and social welfare. Prevention, Care, and Treatment In this third decade of the epidemic, there is still neither a cure nor vaccine for AIDS. Life-prolonging drugs have become more affordable and accessible, yet treatment is still largely unavailable to most people who need it in developing countries.

As of June 2005, out of the 6.5 million people needing treatment in these countries, only an estimated 1 million were receiving it. While antiretroviral treatment prolongs the lives of many AIDS patients, it does not cure AIDS. More than 50 HIV vaccine candidates have undergone clinical trials since 1987 and researchers continue to develop strategies for improving defences against the virus. Despite this progress, a safe and effective vaccine is years away. As HIV continues to spread, prevention remains the backbone of programs to curb the epidemic for the foreseeable future. However, there is a need for more comprehensive programs that encompass prevention, care, treatment, and support interventions. Comprehensive prevention programs for people living with HIV include:

— General education about the risk of sexual transmission.
— Support for low-risk behaviour, including condom use.
— Diagnosis and treatment of STIs.
— Counselling and testing for HIV.
— Preventing mother-to-child transmission.
— Ensuring the safety of blood and blood products.
— Needle exchange programs.
— Reducing the stigma attached to HIV and AIDS.

Comprehensive care and treatment programs include antiretroviral therapy, prevention and treatment of opportunistic infections, palliative and home-based care, psychosocial support, post exposure prophylaxis (primarily for exposure to HIV as a result of rape or needle stick), and support for orphans and children of people living with AIDS.

Prevention and Care

The various components of the prevention and care continuum are mutually reinforcing. The availability of HIV care and treatment services can be a powerful incentive for people to seek counselling and testing. Without such services, people have little incentive to learn their HIV status. Counselling provides an opportunity to educate infected people about the importance of and methods for preventing the infection of others.

Experts often cite counselling and testing for HIV—at AIDS clinics or as routinely offered by health providers—as a crucial entry point for effective prevention, treatment, and care. Access to care and treatment also helps reduce the stigma associated with HIV infection, encourages more people to get tested for HIV, and may promote behaviour change. But convincing people to change their behaviour is difficult, especially if they believe that they are not personally at risk or that they can be successfully treated for AIDS. Studies in more developed countries have shown that some people practice high-risk sexual behaviour when they know that effective AIDS therapies are available.

Prevention programs are much more likely to be successful if they involve policymakers and community lead-12. Public policies that support HIV-prevention programs enable people to protect themselves. Successful prevention programs also address the factors that put individuals, families, and communities at risk of HIV infection and that increase their vulnerability to infection. Prevention programs are effective only if they can reach the majority of people most at risk, especially young adults and marginalised groups such as sex workers, men who have sex with men, injecting drug users, and the sexual partners of those infected. Successful programs are tailored to focus on the main modes of transmission in any given community.

Sexual transmission is the primary mode of transmission in most countries, especially in less developed regions, but transfusions of contaminated blood, injecting drug use, and mother-to-child transmission are responsible for up to 30 percent of all global HIV infections. If prevention activities are focused on these groups when an epidemic is localised, the prevalence of HIV in the general population can remain low. However, even when the epidemic is localised, there is still a need for prevention programs for the general population.

In sub-Saharan Africa, successful prevention programs focus on preventing transmission through heterosexual intercourse, from mothers-to-children, and through contaminated blood. In Southeast Asia, the primary focus is preventing transmission through sex and injecting drug use. In Eastern Europe, the emphasis is on transmission via injecting drug use. In Latin America and in high-income countries, prevention efforts need to encompass homosexual and heterosexual transmission, as well as transmission through injecting drug use.

Preventing Sexual Transmission

The most common mode of HIV transmission is sexual contact. Men and women with multiple sexual partners, including sex workers and their clients, men who have sex with men, and youth are the groups at highest risk of sexual transmission.

The most effective prevention programs promote or include interventions such as abstinence, delay in sexual debut and mutual fidelity, as well as limiting the number of sexual partners; consistent and correct condom use; STI treatment; counselling and testing, and a supportive social and policy environment. A program that focuses only on a few components may not serve the entire population and will have minimal national impact. The most effective mix of these components depends on cultural context as well as specific prevention needs and characteristics of key groups. Effective programs also consider the economic, social, and cultural factors that may affect individual's behaviour.

Sexual debut at a young age, multiple partners, inter-generation sex, STI infection, and unprotected sex are HIV risk factors that can be mediated through behaviour change. These changes require education about modes of HIV transmission, education on how to delay onset of sexual debut, strategies to eliminate high-risk sex or adopt safer behaviours or seek services, and access to supplies or services needed for protection.

Male circumcision is expected to become an important additional tool in reducing the risk of acquiring HIV. Negotiation skills and empowerment are also important so people, especially women and girls, can protect themselves.

Abstinence is the prevention method emphasised in programming directed at youth, the demographic with the highest rate of new infections. Strategies to promote abstinence include changing social norms, sex education, and peer education. "Secondary abstinence" among people who have had sex can also reduce risk of HIV. Abstinence-only programs have been criticised for being unresponsive to the needs of people who are raped, economically dependent on sex work, or are in unions with an HIV-infected spouse or partner.

While abstinence and mutual monogamy with an un infected partner are effective preventive behaviours, they may be difficult to maintain. Consistent condom use has been very effective in protecting against the transmission of HIV and other STIs in people who are sexually active. In married or monogamous couples, one common barrier to condom use is a concern that it implies infidelity. Teaching strategies to negotiate condom use can increase acceptability to sexual partners while addressing these concerns. In Thailand and Cambodia, commercial sex establishments with condom-use policies reduced HIV transmission among sex workers and their clients, as well as in the general population. Consistent condom use reduces HIV transmission in zero discordant couples (in which only one partner is HIV positive) approximately sixfold.

Condoms also prevent STIs, which may contribute up to a tenfold increase in susceptibility to HIV. STIs such as syphilis or gonorrhoea can be treated with antibiotics to reduce this risk, while infections that cannot be cured—genital herpes, for example—may be controlled by cyclophoria or other antiviral medications. Even without medication, people with incurable STIs benefit from medical attention by receiving counselling on safer sex, partner notification strategies, and general health information. STI services can address both biological and behaviour risk factors in sexually active people through treatment and counselling.

The Brazil HIV/AIDS program has demonstrated that education about and access to condom use among young people are effective. Condom use at first sexual intercourse among young Brazilians increased from less than 5 percent in 1986 to 63 percent in 2003. Ongoing research has demonstrated that male circumcision can protect against HIV infection. Circumcision is not practised in many areas of eastern and southern Africa, which may be one reason for the high HIV prevalence in those regions. A clinical trial in South Africa found that circumcised men were 61 percent less likely to become infected with HIV than men who were not circumcised. In Rakai, Uganda, a recent study has demonstrated that male circumcision reduced HIV infection in female partners by 30 percent. If subsequent studies confirm these findings, male circumcision could become an important tool for the control of HIV.

There are several factors that may reduce the risk of HIV infection in circumcised men. The absence of foreskin can shorten drying time following sexual contact, which reduces the life expectancy of HIV and the amount of time the skin is in direct contact with the virus. The total surface area of the penis and the number of target cells, abundant on the foreskin, are reduced through circumcision.

Several studies have indicated that most adult men would undergo circumcision if they believed it protected them against HIV infection. Male circumcision may prove effective in reducing HIV infection, but it is not a panacea for prevention. Circumcision does not The Global Challenge of HIV and AIDS offer complete protection from HIV. A comprehensive prevention approach including education about abstinence, being faithful, and condom use should be available to all men, circumcised or not, to prevent the spread of the virus.

A UN Work Plan on Male Circumcision is developing technical guidance on programmatic, social, and clinical issues concerning the expansion of male circumcision services. These guidelines will assist country program managers to ensure that male circumcisions are being performed appropriately while minimising the risk of clinical complications, the stigma and discrimination against circumcised and uncircumcised men, and to avoid undermining other HIV-prevention strategies.

Preventing HIV Transmission via and Injecting Drug

There are an estimated 13 million injecting drug users worldwide, and as many as 3.3 million are infected with HIV. Between 5 percent and 11 percent of all AIDS cases are related to injecting drug use, which is a major mode of HIV transmission in southern and Eastern Europe, most of Asia and North America, and parts of South America. Injecting drug use is also an important source of infection in North Africa and the Middle East. Transmission in injecting drug users is primarily a result of sharing contaminated needles. However, all drug users, injecting or non-injecting, can play a role in spreading HIV to the general population through sexual transmission, especially users who trade sex for drugs or money, or who engage in risky sexual behaviours when impaired by drugs.

The spread of HIV in people using drugs is often rapid and difficult to control. The underground culture and social stigma attached to drug use and HIV make this population difficult to reach. Studies show, however, that given the appropriate information and opportunity, many injecting drug users will change their drug-using and sexual behaviours to protect themselves and their partners from HIV. Education programs have succeeded in reducing HIV transmission among people who inject drugs in several developed countries, including Australia, Canada, and the

United States. Harm reduction models, such as needle exchange programs, can minimise the use of contaminated needles. Concerns that needle exchange programs increase the frequency of drug use have not been realised. Methadone and buprenorphine treatment can reduce dependency on illegal drugs, thereby reducing high-risk behaviours. Ensuring condom availability and teaching correct condom use can curb unprotected sex. STI and other health care services reduce risk while creating opportunities for counselling or referrals to drug treatment programs. For drug users living with HIV or AIDS, care, treatment, and support services can be integrated into drug treatment programs.

Preventing Transmission via HIV-Infected Blood

Some of the first people identified with HIV acquired the infection from infected blood products in high-income countries. Thousands of people were infected through blood products in the 1980s, but the number of such infections plummeted when tests to screen blood and blood donors became widely used. In more developed countries, the dramatic reduction of HIV transmission from blood is one of the greatest success stories in the battle against the epidemic. However, contaminated blood continues to cause between 5 percent and 10 percent of new HIV infections worldwide and is especially problematic in low-income countries that have inadequate health infrastructures.

Unsanitary blood collection practices infected thousands of villagers in rural China in the 1990s. Preventing the transmission of HIV through blood and blood products involves establishing a well-organised blood transfusion service; exercising universal precautions during blood collection and handling; recruiting safe blood donors, using effective blood tests for HIV and other infectious diseases; ensuring appropriate use of blood and blood products, including avoiding unnecessary transfusions; and preventing health problems, such as anaemia, that require blood transfusions.

Preventing Iatrogenic Transmission

Unsafe medical practices contribute to iatrogenic transmission—the unintentional transmission of HIV by medical personnel. Health care workers, particularly in rural areas, may not receive adequate training in universal safety precautions. Ineffective sterilisation techniques and poor sanitation practices in medical facilities can expose health workers and patients to blood and other body fluids containing HIV. Improper disposal of used syringes, needles, and other medical equipment is another potential hazard.

Cultural expectations of medical care may increase the risk of iatrogenic HIV transmission. In some areas, a medical visit is considered incomplete without an injection—often unnecessary injections of antibiotics, vitamins, analgesics, or chloroquine. HIV can survive in needles that are used for intramuscular and subcutaneous injections and pose a risk for HIV transmission if reused. In 2000, the reuse of injection equipment accounted for an estimated 5 percent of new HIV infections. Transmission between provider and patient is also a risk in health care settings. Health care workers are commonly exposed to blood or infectious products in the course of routine work. Practising universal precautions, such as wearing gloves and masks, consistently allows for non-stigmatising care for all people, regardless of patient or provider's HIV status.

Traditional healers are a significant source of care in many regions of the world, and many engage in activities that could expose them or their patients to HIV. Some practitioners believe the source of HIV is not biologically rooted, making precautions seem unnecessary. Contact with contaminated equipment may occur through common cultural practices including scarification, male and female circumcision, and tattooing.

Preventing Mother-to-Child Transmission

The great majority (90 percent) of HIV-positive children acquired the virus from their mother. The risk of a mother transmitting the virus to her baby is around 15 percent to 30 percent—a risk that increases to as high as 45 percent with prolonged breast-feeding.. Approximately 800,000 infants are newly infected with HIV annually, nearly all in developing countries; 90 percent of infected children live in sub-Saharan Africa. Risk of transmission is affected by factors related to the virus, the mother, the delivery process, the baby, and how the infant is fed.

During pregnancy and delivery, the mother's health, disruption of the placental barrier, pre-term delivery, and haemorrhage are significant predictors of the child's infection. After delivery, breast-feeding is the most important risk factor. Without treatment, an estimated one in every seven infants breast-fed by an HIV-positive mother becomes infected through breast milk.

Current strategies for preventing mother-to-child transmission include primary prevention of HIV in girls and women; counselling and testing in pregnant women; family planning services to reduce pregnancy in infected mothers; preventive antiretroviral drug therapy; follow-up care and treatment for mother and infant; and nutritional counselling and breast-milk substitutes, if appropriate. The most effective drug therapy tested so far is long-course HAART, which can reduce transmission to 2 percent. HAART's complexity and cost have limited its use in resource-poor settings. Shorter, simpler, and less costly regimens are available.

The most practical and least expensive (US$4 per dose) of these options is nevirapine. Single doses can be given at birth to both the mother and infant. Boehringer-Ingelheim, the company that manufactures nevirapine, has made the drug available for free in less developed countries to prevent mother-to-child transmission. But many women are developing a resistance to nevirapine and similar drugs, making them less useful in the future. A recent study reported that up to 69 percent of women may have resistance to this class of drugs one to four months after nevirapine prophylactic treatment is discontinued. WHO is currently reviewing the policy implications of this finding and is likely to recommend a combination of HAART for the prevention of mother-to-child transmission.

Based on trial data from Zambia, WHO, UNICEF, and UN AIDS recommend the use of cotrimoxizole to reduce mother-to-child transmission. In regions where children under 18 months of age cannot be reliably tested, cotrimoxizole prophylaxis is recommended for all children born to HIV-infected mothers. Cotrimoxizole can also prevent and treat Pneumocystis pneumonia, as well as other opportunistic infections, in children infected with HIV.

Helping Orphans and Vulnerable Children Because HIV is infectious, there is a high risk that a child who loses one parent to AIDS will lose the other one as well. While the increasing availability of treatment will slow the rate of increase in children orphaned by AIDS, the number of orphans and vulnerable children will continue to rise for the foreseeable future. When children are left without parents, communities must respond to their needs to avoid their exploitation, ensure their welfare, and promote healthy development.

Most of the children orphaned by AIDS in sub-Saharan Africa are cared for by extended family members. Some of these caretakers are HIV-infected or are responsible for other family members living with HIV and AIDS, which can create both financial and emotional burdens. Many extended families are unable to provide the school fees, food, and health care costs of additional children. In many high-HIV-prevalence regions, community-based organisations help families meet the needs of the orphan households through material, financial, emotional, or psychosocial support to the children and the caretaker.

Community support for families is more cost-effective than other options that countries are trying, including building or expanding orphanages. While orphanages can meet the immediate; urgent needs of an orphaned child, they are not the best long-term situation. Orphanages are expensive to operate, often fail to meet the developmental needs of the child, and can isolate children from community support systems.

MANAGING HIV AND AIDS

In 2005, an estimated 6.5 million people needed antiretroviral treatment; only about 15 percent—1 million people—had access to it. In sub-Saharan Africa, around 11 percent of those in need of treatment were receiving it. The main reasons for this shortfall include the high cost of treatment; procurement challenges; inadequate health infrastructure, including a lack of health care providers; insufficient political commitment at the national level; inadequate or uncertain financial resources; and the persistent stigma that often prevents people from seeking care.

The clinical objectives of antiretroviral therapy are to suppress the replication of the virus and restore immune function of the body; limit the likelihood of viral resistance to antiretroviral drugs; and reduce HIV-related morbidity and mortality.

Since the introduction of entire travellers in 1996, drug therapy has transformed HIV from a progressive terminal illness to a manageable chronic disease. Drugs, although they cannot cure it. The current antiretroviral drugs—which fall into three main classes—work by blocking enzymes that are important for the replication and functioning of HIV in the body. A newer class of entire travellers—entry inhibitors—works differently: It fights HIV after it has infected the immune system. Entry inhibitors offer hope to people who have developed resistance to current HIV medications. Combining drugs from different classes is the most effective therapy for thwarting AIDS, because the virus can develop resistance to drugs used individually. A similar multi-drug approach is used to treat cancer and TB.

Recent studies have shown that low-cost regimens can prevent some of the opportunistic infections that commonly occur with HIV, including TB and Pneumomycosis carinae pneumonia (PCP), and other major causes of illness, such as non-typhoid salmonella infections and cerebral toxoplasmosis. Preventive therapy for TB would be especially effective in sub-Saharan Africa, where TB is a major cause of death in HIV-positive individuals. Using cotrimoxazole to treat PCP patients who have HIV can significantly reduce hospitalisation and mortality from other bacterial opportunistic infections. Fungal infections, a major cause of illness and death in HIV-positive individuals, respond to preventive therapy with fluconazole. These simple preventive therapies could reduce illness in people living with HIV. Their relatively low cost means they could reach a much wider population than more expensive antiretroviral drugs. However, further research is needed on who should receive them for how long and how the therapies affect drug resistance in the long term.

The broad goal of clinical care (including drug therapy) is to improve the quality of life of people living with HIV by improving access to comprehensive prevention and care programs. Evidence from both developed and developing countries has shown that antiretroviral therapy can dramatically prolong the lives of persons living with HIV, enabling them to remain productive members of their community, support their families, and raise their children.

Clinical care programs can also help reduce the number of orphans and vulnerable children by prolonging the lives of parents; reduce mother-to-child transmission; and lessen the risk of sexual transmission because of lower viral load in body fluids. Care programs also combat stigma and discrimination associated with HIV and AIDS.

Palliative care is an important component of comprehensive care for people living with HIV. Many people experience pain, diarrhoea, nausea, cough, shortness of breath, fatigue, fever, and confusion, as well as damaging psychosocial stress associated with illness, stigma, and end-of-life issues. Preventing these symptoms through palliative care prevents pain and unnecessary visits to health care facilities and allows people with AIDS to remain as active as possible in their community. Traditional healing, local remedies, and a mix of support services can also play a significant role. Training home-based care providers, community volunteers, or family members in palliative care can enhance the quality of life of people living with AIDS.

Home-based care offers a variety of benefits to people living with HIV and AIDS, as well as their families, especially to people with uncertain access to health care facilities. Home-based care providers have a unique opportunity to identify vulnerable children in the household who may need services.

Access to Treatment

A recent and dramatic rise in global funding, aggressive international initiatives, and lower costs of entire travellers have increased access to treatment in several countries. The most successful national treatment programs in developing countries are in Brazil and Botswana. Brazil's treatment program demonstrates the importance of political commitment, adequate national resources, the close involvement of civil society, and comprehensive prevention and treatment programs. Brazil's program also shows the considerable level of resources needed to provide universal access and comprehensive prevention and treatment services.

The Brazilian government provided nearly 90 percent of these resources. The commitment of huge resources has certainly worked for Brazil—a middle-income country—but most developing countries may not be able to afford to provide free treatment for everyone in need. The African Comprehensive HIV/AIDS Partnerships (ACHAP) in Botswana program is a joint effort between the government of Botswana, the Bill & Melinda Gates Foundation, and the Merck Company Foundation/Merck Company Inc. that has dramatically improved national access to treatment. The program was launched in 2000 and reached 42,000 with antiretroviral drug therapy (56 percent of those in need) by December 2004.

The antiretroviral drugs used most often to treat AIDS belong to three major classes: nucleoside reverse transcriptase inhibitors (NRTIs), non-nucleoside reverse transcriptase inhibitors (NNRTIs), and protease inhibitors. A fourth class of drugs called entry inhibitors (including fusion inhibitors) is now available. Entry inhibitors work by preventing HIV from entering T-cells. Healthy Tcells are crucial for the body's defense against pathogens like HIV.

Treatment coverage continues to improve in several countries as a result of increased resources from the U.S. President's Emergency Plan for AIDS Relief and the Global Fund to Fight AIDS, Tuberculosis, and Malaria. The President's Emergency Plan expects to reach 2 million people in 15 focus countries by 2008. The Global Fund has committed nearly US$2.5 billion to HIV/AIDS and estimates that more than 1.8 million people will be on entire travellers through grants.

Despite these efforts, the vast majority of people living with HIV will go without effective treatment for several years to come. Many people living with HIV lack access to health facilities and cannot afford to pay reduced, but still substantial, co-payments for treatment. Many developing countries do not have the financial resources and infrastructure to support a large-scale HIV treatment program. The most neglected populations for treatment are often children, women, rural important initiatives expanded the arsenal of weapons in the battle against HIV and AIDS.

Fund to Fight against AIDS

In 2001, the UN created the Global Fund to Fight AIDS, Tuberculosis and Malaria, with a target of US$9 billion to support integrated approaches to prevention, care, support, and treatment. The establishment of the fund helped refocus attention not only on HIV, but also on two other important threats to international health: tuberculosis (TB) and malaria. The Global Fund disburses funds to implementing agencies, a diverse group representing multiple sectors of society. Donors to the Global Fund include the governments of more than 50 countries, as well as foundations, corporations, and private donors. The Global Fund also finances programs for malaria and TB, diseases that are rampant in many high-HIV-prevalence countries.

The Global Fund has committed US$2.5 billion to HIV prevention, care, and treatment programs in countries around the world. Between 2001 and 2005, the Global Fund provided treatment for 220,000 people with HIV, more than 1.1 million people with malaria, and 600,000 people with TB. If fully funded, the Global Fund aims to provide 1.8 million people with antiretroviral therapy (ART) and 62 million people with voluntary counselling and testing, and to support more than 1 million orphans with medical services, education, and community care.

In 2003, the U.S. President's Emergency Plan for AIDS Relief was initiated as a five-year, US$15 billion global initiative to fight HIV and AIDS outside the United States. The Emergency Plan has a strong emphasis on care and treatment, with 55 percent of funds devoted to treatment, 15 percent for palliative care, 20 percent for HIV/AIDS prevention (with at least 33 percent for promoting abstinence until marriage), and 10 percent for helping orphans and vulnerable children. Fifteen focus countries (Botswana, Cote devour, Ethiopia, Guyana, Haiti, Kenya, Mozambique, Namibia, Nigeria, Rwanda, South Africa, Tanzania, Uganda, Zambia, and Vietnam) receive Emergency Plan funds. ART has been provided to more than 235,000 people living with HIV; more than 1.1 million have been reached with essential care services. Treatment may increase at a faster rate since funds can now be spent on much less expensive generic antiretroviral drugs (ARVs), following a ruling by the U.S. Food and Drug Administration in 2005.

The 3 by 5 Initiative was launched by the World Health Organisation (WHO) and UN AIDS in September 2003. Its goal: To provide antiretroviral drugs to 3 million people living with AIDS in developing countries by the end of 2005, and to reach at least half of the people in need. The UN AIDS/WHO initiative relied on partnerships with the Global Fund, the Emergency Plan, the World Bank, national governments, and non-governmental organisations (NGOs). By mid-2005, approximately 1 million people in the developing world had access to ARVs, 2 million below the target number. Fourteen low- to middle-income countries surpassed the 3 by 5 goal of providing ARVs to more than 50 percent of those in need. However, ART reached only about 15 percent of all those in need, well below the target of 50 percent.

The 3 by 5 goals proved too ambitious, given the many barriers to rapidly scaling up ART, especially in poor countries. Some countries lacked the political commitment needed for rapidly increasing access to ART. Bottlenecks in supply, limited human capacity, high drug prices, and poor infrastructure within many developing countries were also major obstacles.

Funding from donors was often unpredictable and insufficient, and technical assistance from WHO and other agencies could not overcome the weak infrastructure in many countries. Although the 3 by 5 goals were not met, the plan did help many countries deliver ART to more people, improve health infrastructure, and, most important, demonstrate the feasibility of treating large numbers of people living with AIDS in the developing world.

The Global Challenge of HIV and AIDS residents, and marginalised populations such as injecting drug users and sex workers. Drug therapy programs need to closely involve civil society, especially community-based organisations of people living with HIV, and ensure equal access to clinical care for women, children, and other vulnerable and marginalised populations. Treatment for children with HIV poses special challenges. Without treatment, at least one-half of infected infants will die before their second birthday; yet even determining the HIV status of infants is difficult. The antibody tests used in developing countries cannot detect HIV infection in children less than 18 months of age. The more costly antigen tests that can measure infection in very young children are rarely available. Children are also vulnerable because they usually cannot advocate for their own health care and depend on parents or guardians to initiate medical visits. Children also have limited treatment options—most AIDS drugs formulations are not appropriate for children—and treatment regimens must be constantly monitored because effective doses change as children grow.

Only about 5 percent of an estimated 700,000 children in need of antiretroviral therapy received it in 2005.

Expanding Counselling and Testing

Counselling and testing services for HIV have long been a component of HIV prevention and care programs in more developed countries and are proving to be a cost-effective way of reducing risky behaviours and of leading patients to other services. A study of data from Kenya, Tanzania, and Trinidad documented a 43 percent reduction in unprotected sex among people who received voluntary counselling and testing (VCT) for HIV. Counselling and testing programs involve raising community awareness, pre- and post-test counselling, psychological support, and referral to relevant services. HIV counselling helps people cope with personal stress and make decisions related to HIV.

It enables an individual or couple to evaluate their risk of contracting or transmitting HIV and helps them avoid it. Counselling helps people deal with the stigma and discrimination associated with HIV. The very act of being tested, for example, may have negative consequences in communities where HIV-positive people are stigmatised.

Despite their importance, counselling and testing services tend to be of limited quality and coverage in less developed countries. A lack of trained staff, concerns about confidentiality, stigma and discrimination, clients' lack of knowledge about services, and limited resources are some of the reasons why VCT programs are inadequate or under used.

Many countries are increasing the availability and use of testing and counselling services by shifting from voluntary counselling and testing, in which a person goes to a health facility for the primary purpose of receiving an HIV test, to routine testing, in which all patients arriving at a facility are routinely offered an HIV test. Tests with same-day results also increase use, because they eliminate the need for patients to return to a health clinic to receive their results—and more patients will actually learn their HIV status.

Several countries have successfully increased counselling and testing services. Botswana, one of the highest prevalence countries, was the first in Africa to routinely offer HIV testing in both public and private clinics. A growing body of evidence suggests that making HIV testing part of standard care reduces the stigma associated with the disease and increases the number choosing to be tested. Routine testing, mass media campaigns promoting the value of knowing HIV status, and learning the benefits and the wide availability of treatment, have dramatically increased the use of counselling and testing services in Botswana.

In Kenya, the introduction of routine testing (with the option of refusal) in antenatal care clinics doubled the use of testing and counselling from 37 percent to 75 percent in one month. Lesotho has taken the concept of routine testing one step further to community-based door-to-door testing in their KYS (Know Your Status) campaign. This is an attempt to significantly boost the number of people who know their HIV status. Currently, only 9 percent of men and 13 percent of women are aware of their status in a country with an adult HIV prevalence of 30 percent. The program includes training community leaders as prevention and treatment supporters, involving people living with HIV in adherence and prevention activities, and recruiting 7,500 health workers for counselling and testing.

Challenges in HIV Control

Despite major medical and technological breakthroughs and advances, the AIDS epidemic continues its relentless spread in many resource-poor settings. AIDS continues to be one of the most devastating and important global public health and developmental problems. However, HIV and AIDS control must compete with other emergencies, including civil strife, natural disasters, and continuing threats of emerging infectious diseases such as Ebola, SARS, and avian influenza. Three key challenges for the future are controlling further spread of the epidemic in infants and young adults; treating, caring for, and supporting the neglected millions of people living with HIV; and mitigating the epidemic's impact on the millions of people affected by AIDS in resource-constrained countries. To meet these challenges, the international community and national governments and civil society need to take a number of steps, including:

— Increasing resources available for comprehensive prevention, care, treatment, and support services.

— Ensuring that prevention remains the backbone of AIDS control programs, even with expanded treatment access.

— Improving the health infrastructure and capacity for delivery of services.

— Improving technologies for the treatment and prevention of AIDS.

— Reducing poverty, illiteracy, and other social, economic, and political actors that increase vulnerability to infection.

— Reducing the stigma and discrimination against those living with HIV.

Improving Resources for HIV Programs

Resources available for HIV and AIDS have increased from US$300 million in 1996 to US$10 billion in 2006. Despite this increase, UN AIDS estimates that US$22 billion is needed by 2008 to ensure an adequate response to the expanding AIDS epidemic. The response would include low-cost HAART, treatment of opportunistic infections, and support for orphans and vulnerable children. Providing such support will likely require major increases in national government allocations; greater support from the private sector; and substantial increases in international assistance.

Prevention and treatment programs for the AIDS pandemic have been inadequate, small-scale, and fragmented in most countries, particularly in less developed regions. With few exceptions, the efforts have failed to slow the spread of the virus or to reduce the damaging effects of the pandemic. However, public health and policy experts cite a number of strategies that could help meet the need for an expanded and comprehensive response. An effective response should include strategic planning, a multi-sectorial approach, and the active involvement of non-governmental organisations (NGOs).

Ideally, HIV programs should also include state-of-the-art technical strategies; adequate distribution of resources at the community level; development of human capacity as well as technical and operational competence; and better management and supply of drugs and commodities. Program planners also need to anticipate the costs of expanded coverage, program evaluation, and future technological developments. An expanded and comprehensive response also requires improving public- and private-sector capacity to expand care and treatment services, including new technologies such as HAART and vaccines. But the most critical challenge is the effective application of current technologies on a large enough scale to curb the epidemic, improve access to care and treatment, reduce stigma and discrimination for persons living with HIV, and support and protect orphans and vulnerable children.

INTEGRATING PREVENTION AND TREATMENT

Programs to prevent HIV transmission often compete with programs to treat people suffering from AIDS for scarce resources and political support. But new mathematical models confirm there is a asynergy between prevention and treatment efforts, and that both are crucial for controlling the AIDS epidemic. Successful prevention programs help reduce the number of new infections and ultimately the number of people who need treatment. Successful treatment programs not only prolong the lives of people living with HIV but will also slow the spread of HIV by lowering the viral load of people with the virus.

Effective care and treatment programs can reduce AIDS deaths, but a long-term decline will be driven by preventing new infections. Treatment programs can also enhance prevention efforts by reducing stigma. Scaling up both treatment and prevention efforts could avert about one-half of new HIV infections and prevent more than one-fourth of AIDS-related deaths over the next two decades.

SEARCH FOR A VACCINE

A safe, stable, efficacious, affordable, and accessible HIV vaccine would significantly enhance HIV prevention and help control the global epidemic. HIV vaccine development and testing has greatly accelerated over the last few years, notably with the Global HIV Vaccine Initiative, an alliance of independent organisations trying to accelerate the development of a vaccine by sharing information and working cooperatively.

HIV researchers say that an ideal vaccine is at least seven to 10 years away because of many scientific, ethical, legal, and financial stumbling blocks. HIV infection and the human immune response are highly complex, and research and development are costly and time-consuming. In addition, there are no appropriate animal tests or alternate models for investigating possible vaccines. Human clinical trials always raise ethical and legal issues, especially when trials involve a fatal infectious agent like HIV. More than 30 HIV vaccine candidates were in clinical trials as of mid-2005.

One large-scale efficacy trial completed in 2003 demonstrated that people are willing to participate in vaccine trials. The search for a vaccine is not limited to people living in high-income countries; nine developing countries are currently conducting or preparing to conduct HIV vaccine trials. The full participation of people living in the hardest-hit areas is important to ensure that a vaccine is effective against different sub-types of the virus. One of the greatest barriers to an effective vaccine is the lack of financial incentive to produce it. Current investment in HIV vaccine development is around US$682 million per year, less than 1 percent of spending on all health product development. Private-sector involvement in vaccine development has been limited and only four pharmaceutical companies currently have vaccines in clinical trials. Governments, small biotechnology companies, and NGOs have broadened ongoing research, but more resources are needed to hasten the process.

If an effective HIV vaccine becomes available, the international community will need to address new challenges, including determining who will benefit the most from the vaccine and ensuring equitable access; understanding behavioural issues raised by a vaccine; developing new tests to differentiate between vaccine-induced and active HIV infection; and raising sufficient resources to deliver the vaccine.

Developing Microbicide

Millions of women around the world are not able to protect

themselves from HIV infection. Most prevention strategies rely on abstinence, monogamy, condom use, fewer sexual partners, and treatment of STIs. However, many women are powerless to demand condom use or refuse sex. A woman may risk HIV infection through other sexual partners her husband may have had. Microbicide would give women much more control over their risk of infection. A microbicide is a substance—usually a gel, cream, or suppository—that can be applied to the vagina or rectum to prevent or substantially reduce the transmission of STIs or HIV. Microbicide can kill or immobilise the pathogen by creating a barrier between the pathogen and the vagina or rectum or by preventing the pathogen from replicating once it has entered the cells.

A woman could use a microbicide if her partner does not use a condom, as an adjunct to condom use, and as backup protection in the event of condom failure. Microbicide could be applied before sexual intercourse and without the knowledge of the sexual partner. The search for a microbicide suffered a major setback when a study in Cameroun showed that nonoxynol-9 (N-9), a widely used spermicide, did not protect users against HIV. It may even increase the risk slightly when used frequently.

About 30 microbicide are in various stages of development in 2006. Five of these are in or about to enter large-scale clinical trials. The development of an effective and affordable microbicide would place HIV prevention in the hands of women and has the potential to avert between 2.5 million and 3.7 million infections over three years. The antiretroviral drug ten favour may also be an effective pre-exposure prophylactic agent. Ten favour can be taken once daily by mouth and has few side effects in people living with HIV.

Research in un infected animals has shown that ten favour may reduce the risk of HIV infection if taken prior to exposure to the virus. Clinical trials in Cambodia, Nigeria, and Cameroun to evaluate the effectiveness of ten favour in preventing human infection were halted in 2004 and 2005 because of pressure from activist groups about ethical concerns. Despite these setbacks, new trials have begun to determine if ten favour can effectively protect people from HIV infection.

Protecting Human Rights

Human rights protections are critical for reducing vulnerability to HIV, protecting the dignity of persons affected by the virus, and sharing medical advances with less developed countries. Women's rights are especially relevant to the fight against HIV. Combating gender inequality tackles one of the root causes of the epidemic: women's inability to protect themselves from HIV. AIDS experts have outlined several ways to enhance women's rights to reduce their vulnerability and exposure to HIV, including promoting sexual responsibility among boys and men, developing female-controlled prevention methods such as microbicide, and increasing women's economic opportunities.

Violations of the rights of those living with HIV have been documented worldwide and have included denial of medical care, breaches of the right to privacy, restriction of HIV information for certain populations, and discrimination in employment and housing. Under international law, governments are obligated to respect, protect, and fulfil the human rights of people vulnerable to HIV, those living with HIV/AIDS, and those affected by the disease.

The right of people in less developed countries to have access to life-saving drugs is a crucial human rights issue in the context of HIV. AIDS activists argue that lack of resources at the individual and national levels, inadequate health infrastructure, and protecting pharmaceutical companies' investments and patents are no longer acceptable reasons for denying treatment access to AIDS patients in less developed countries. Human rights groups, people living with HIV, and civil and political leaders have joined in the call to make HIV related treatments available and affordable to less developed countries. As a result, prices of antiretroviral drugs have dropped dramatically, therapies have been offered at cost or free to less developed countries, resources are becoming available to provide treatment and care, and pharmaceutical patent rights are being challenged. Despite these changes, the vast majority of people living with HIV in less developed countries will not have access to treatment in the foreseeable future.

9

Population Problems

The present is unexpectedly a critical time for population change and policy. We are little more than half way through the great population growth spurt that began in the middle of the twentieth century, but developed-country governments seem to be losing interest in the issue. This loss of interest may have a significant demographic impact. The probable reasons for the declining interest are a vague belief that the present demographic change has a momentum of its own, a reaction to the International Conference on Population and Development (ICPD) in Cairo in 1994 which may misinterpret the complex document that came out of that meeting, and a preoccupation with below-replacement-level fertility in the developed world.

Huge population growth is not now past history. United Nations estimates and medium projections show a world population numbering 2.5 billion in 1950, 6.1 billion in 2000 and 9.3 billion in 2050. The next half-century will see almost as many people added to the world's population as the last half-century, and thereafter there may be one or two billion more people before growth comes to a halt. Global fertility decline is believed to have traversed over four-fifths of the journey from a total fertility rate of 5.0 in 1950 to 2.1 in 2050.

But because of population growth momentum and an ever-expanding base population, the additions to world population did not peak until the 1990s at around 80 million per year, and are only a little below that now. There are two main messages for future-glazers and policy makers. The first is that projections are far from certain. The second is that projections are necessarily based on past experience–including past policy experience–and, if this changes, then the projections must do so too. The lack of certainty is shown by the fact that for 2050 the United Nations provides, in addition to the Medium Projection of 9.322 billion, a Low Projection of 7.866 billion and a High Projection of 10.934 billion.

The High Projection is over three billion or almost 40 per cent above the Low Projection. Another recent projection, by Lutz and others, provides a 2050 median figure of 8.797 billion, with an 80 per cent probability of it falling between 7.347 and 10.443 billion. The latter projection's "most likely" figure for 2050 is about half a billion below that of the United Nations but still implies huge growth and great uncertainty about its magnitude.

Most analysts have preferred during recent years to employ the United Nations Medium Projection because it has proved in these years to be remarkably accurate. This period of near-certainty may be passing. Two years after its release in 1999 of the 1998 projections, the United Nations produced revised figures raising the 2050 Medium estimate by 413 million people, 96 per cent of the difference being attributable to new figures for Africa and Asia, mostly in sub-Saharan Africa and South Asia. The United Nations Population Division said that 59 per cent of the upward adjustment was explained by countries (mostly in sub-Saharan Africa) failing to begin fertility declines as early as expected, and 32 per cent was because of greater sluggishness than anticipated in fertility decline in such large countries as Bangladesh, India and Nigeria.

Twentieth-century projections were based on twentieth-century experience, and that was propelled by a near-consensus among powerful donor countries and their citizens about the need to give population control high policy priority and adequate funding. This played a role in developing-country governments adopting population policies that brought down levels of fertility and population growth faster than socioeconomic change alone would have done. It also played a role in the development of contraception suited to large-scale family planning programmes in poor, under educated countries. That consensus is now held with less fervour and this is reflected in funding and First World leadership. The result will almost certainly be slower fertility decline and greater population growth which must be reflected in adequate population projections.

The reasons for the loss of fervour are several. One is the initial success in reducing fertility, and its reflection in United Nations and other statistics. The world is less homogeneous than the reaction to these changes suggested. Fertility decline was persistent in relatively well-off and educated Latin America and in rapidly economically developing parts of East and Southeast Asia. However, there was the potential for problems elsewhere which was often not noted, but which can be observed in the three large countries pinpointed in the most recent United Nations projections as being unexpectedly sluggish. There are many reasons why the fertility transition may be slow in some parts of sub-Saharan Africa.

Among the people there are cultural resistance and among governments a lack of enthusiasm for leadership in the area: for these reasons national family planning programmes are unlikely to be like those of Asia or to have the same effect. There is also a very low level of development, with a high proportion of the population practising subsistence farming. Here extra hands produce extra food, and there will be extra hands where few children go to school. There are 20 countries in sub-Saharan Africa where women still have six or more children and there is little sign of fertility decline. These 20 countries average an infant mortality rate over 150 per thousand, a life expectancy of 45 years, and a per capita gross national income in purchasing power parity of a little over US$850.

Perhaps more significantly, only half their girls of primary school age are in school as are one-third of those of secondary school age (net enrolment ratios). Compared with African countries like Ghana, Kenya and South Africa where there have been marked falls in fertility, their infant mortality rates are two to three times higher, their income levels lower, and their girls' secondary school enrolment level half. Ghana and Kenya laid the foundation of their fertility decline before the African economic crisis which began in the mid-1980s.

Their populations already assumed that children's health could be guarded by modern medicine and that both boys and girls would normally go to school. The subsequent economic crisis and the family financial outlays associated with cost recovery in structural adjustment programmes did not reverse these assumptions but rather convinced many parents that their educational and health expectations could be maintained only if they had children more widely spaced. The poorer countries did not participate in this two-step process but are still beset by few and fee-charging schools and health facilities. They are also facing the beginning of demographic transition in an era of AIDS.

Except in a few, mostly Southern African countries, the African fertility decline is largely an urban phenomenon, since the nature of families, the occupations of adults and the roles of children and expectations for them are very different in the towns from those in the countryside. The slow movers tend to be less urbanised than the countries where fertility decline is taking place, and especially tend to lack big cities. Finally, the higher-fertility countries have often had more immediate concerns than demographic ones, for they include most of sub-Saharan Africa's war-torn countries: Liberia, Sierra Leone, Arteria, Somalia, Uganda, Angola and the Congo Democratic Republic.

Threshold explanations are not now popular, but some explanation of this kind is probably relevant to the situation in the large sluggish countries of South Asia. Bangladesh is probably the prime example, a country where a comparatively expensive and efficient family planning programme, assisted by a marked degree of socioeconomic change, halved its birth rate during the late 1970s and 1980s, only to find that the total fertility rate stagnated around 3.3 through the 1990s. As a consequence, the 2000 74 United Nations Population Projections show it reaching replacement fertility 30 years later than did the 1998 projections.

What had not been previously taken into account is that Bangladesh is the poorest country in the world to have reduced the total fertility rate to 3.3, and it has done so with an infant mortality rate around 70, more than twice the level found in East and Southeast Asia. Bangladesh achieved such low fertility partly by overcoming the problems of purdah by having family planning workers call at every house with the hormonal contraceptive methods favoured in Muslim societies, but ironically donors, with less funding for family planning programmes, are now calling for a greater resort to centralised services and the use of permanent or long-term methods.

India, which has largely funded its own programme, has long sought cheapness with its concentration on sterilisation. It has achieved extraordinary success in its South but to a much lesser extent in its Hindi belt of large northern states (where child mortality is also relatively high). There are similarities in Nigeria where the southern half of the country has paralleled the fertility decline of Ghana and Kenya, but where the poorer, higher-mortality and solidly Muslim north, like neighbouring Niger and Chad, maintains high fertility. ICPD produced a Programme of Action, which, like the product of other international consensuses, was complex, not entirely internally consistent, and easily misunderstood.

It proclaimed that the population movement was no longer to be driven by demographic fears, while at the same time devoting a good deal of space to population growth and its implications. It placed its main emphasis on improving the female situation, especially in the areas of education and reproductive health, while partly justifying or at least noting that this would mean demographic gains in terms of lower child mortality and declining fertility. It sought to achieve reproductive health programmes of a type that the best family planning programmes had always hoped for.

Nevertheless, it discouraged many involved in existing family planning programmes by seeming to condemn what they had hitherto regarded as past successes and by appearing to ask for more than their countries' health services could provide in the foreseeable future. It has almost certainly also confused donors who had not previously considered that the much more expensive national educational and health services warranted the same proportional support as did the family planning programmes.

But Western donor support for family planning programmes has also been weakened by the realisation that the end of demographic transition may not take the form of equal birth and death rates but of below-replacement fertility. This appears to have been achieved already in countries where 44 per cent of the population of the world lives, and began to manifest itself in sustained fertility declines in developed countries from the 1970s. It is partly a product of more girls going to school and more women being in the work force, but it is also the product of forces released by the global effort to limit population growth, namely the invention of better contraception, and the moral support for young couples or young women having few children.

Many policy-makers have now heard the argument that the move to limit population growth in developing countries was either never necessary or no longer necessary. Indeed, the impression has been given that ultimately fertility decline would be a disaster for all countries in that they would move towards a situation where over 30 per cent of the population would be aged, in the sense that they were over 65 years of age, and that this would place an unbearable burden on the working population in supporting old-age pensions and health services by means of high taxes.

The demographic situation is, in fact, much more complex than this, although these complexities have been insufficiently, or unconvincing, spelled out to governments. First, not everyone is convinced that China is below or far below replacement-level fertility, and without its inclusion the proportion of the world's population in this category is halved to 22 per cent. Secondly, very low fertility, with little chance that completed cohort fertility will eventually come close to replacement level as older women continue to have births deferred from their younger years, is largely confined to Central, Eastern and Southern Europe, Japan and South Korea, and possibly Canada, around 750 million or one-eighth of the human race.

Thirdly, population momentum ensures that crisis even in 75 these countries is not imminent. If the present situation continues, it will be one-third of a century before Italy, Spain and Japan experience population decline of half of one per cent per annum and 30 per cent or more of their populations over 65 years, and half a century before Germany does. My point here is that the rich nations should still be primarily concerned with world population growth. By 2050 global population could be 8.9 billion, as the 1998 United Nations Revision Medium Projection calculated, or 9.3 billion as calculated in the 2000 Medium Projection. It could also be the 10.9 billion of the 2000 High Projections or, increasingly unlikely, the 7.9 billion of the 2000 Low Projection.

The peak global populations could range between 9 and 12 billion; or, according to the Lots and others 80 per cent probability projections, between 8 and 12 billion. With regard to the long-term stability of the world's ecosystems and our ability to feed everyone adequately and to give them a reasonably good life, that margin of 3 or 4 billion extra people may be critical. We may well be able to achieve these aims with 12 billion people but we are much more certain of being able to do so with 9 billion, and risking the additional 3 billion does not seem to be a worthwhile experiment.

Just what is likely to happen in the rich countries? The simple answer is that low fertility will continue to characterise these societies. But the situation is far from simple. Because total fertility rates are at present depressed by a continuing deferment of the age of women at marriage and childbearing, most overstate the threat to population replacement. In Europe, Scandinavia, France, Britain, Ireland and perhaps even the Netherlands will probably come close to replacing themselves, as will the United States. In any case, the traditional countries of immigration, the United States, Canada, Australia and New Zealand are unlikely to experience declining population.

On the other hand, much of Southern, Eastern and Central Europe, as well as Japan and South Korea, will face declining population if present trends continue. But two points are important: first, even with present trends, substantial declines are in most cases decades away; second, fertility rates may not remain so low. The reason that fertility may not remain so low is that nationalism is not dead. When real decline is experienced, policies and popular sentiments are likely to turn towards espousing motherhood in a way that may make similar efforts in the 1930s or in Eastern Europe between the 1950s and 1970s look puny.

The post-1960s fertility declines were the result not merely of economic change, but also of a changing attitude to small families and even childlessness, partly arising from the "population explosion" debate. My guess is that in the coming decades we will see the opposite occurring, with popular and governmental lauding of two- and even three-child families, and quite dramatic policy changes to make them possible. The present very low fertility is less the realisation of parental family building aims than the product of the financial difficulties experienced by families in high-consumption societies not having two breadwinners, and by the massive problems faced by mothers in continuing with their education or work or maintaining their position and rate of promotion in employment.

These difficulties arise from insufficient support from governments, employers and husbands. We know that, when Sweden poured money into free preschool support in the 1980s and early 1990s (for gender-equity, not demographic reasons), fertility rose to replacement levels, only to fall again by one-third when these expenditures were cut back as Sweden met the criteria for joining the European Union. The time may come when it is the achievement of motherhood that is linked to getting university scholarships, paying house mortgages and remaining on the fast promotion track.

Such policy and social changes may not be promoted merely by demographic nationalism but also by a variant of the women's movement and by powerful forces aiming at greater gender equity. Italy is already becoming introspective about the causes of its very low fertility as social scientists link it to husbands' failure to share domestic duties and child care, and relate this in turn to men marrying late after years of living as young adults in their parents' homes with mothers teaching them to expect to do nothing in the way of domestic tasks. What is to be hoped is that governments in developed countries can 76 become sufficiently sophisticated to deal with a bipolar world, so that their domestic population policies are separated from their technical aid attitudes to high-fertility countries.

Low fertility is rapidly changing the age structures of developed countries and demographers will continue to monitor this. Whether this portends economic disaster is open to question. The main employed age group, 20-64 years, a more sensible definition for rich countries than 15-64 years, remains a constant proportion of the population at around 56 per cent. The only change is that the burden of dependency shifts from supporting the young to doing the same for the old. This is an important emotional issue in the West where the young tend to be a family responsibility involving direct family expenditure while the old are a state responsibility paid for by family taxation.

This picture is not universal, and, in any case, the changed effect on the national economy is probably not as great as most of the debate has suggested. Moreover, there is a tendency to underrate the efficiency of the modern economy and to overrate its potential for employment. It has shown itself quite capable of producing rising standards of living while up to 10 per cent of the work force is unemployed and another 5-10 per cent prematurely retired. Thus, although the tax base for supporting the aged could be adequately broadened by increasing the retirement age to 70 years, this may not be necessary. In fact, the economy may be at its healthiest if we do not do this, carrying with it, as the policy would, the need to provide unemployment relief for 65-69-year-olds.

Intermediate Fertility Level Countries

hese are defined by the United Nations Population Division as countries with total fertility rates in the range 2.2-4.9. For this analysis, we have defined "large" as being characterised in 2000 by a population of 30 million or more. This group constitutes 18 countries (Algeria, Egypt, Morocco, Sudan, Kenya, South Africa, Mexico, Argentina, Brazil, Columbia, Turkey, Bangladesh, India, Iran, Indonesia, Myanmar, Philippines and Vietnam) with a total population of 2.260 billion or 46 per cent of that of the developing world, 63 per cent without China. India alone constitutes 45 per cent of their population. For analytical purposes we will add three more large high-fertility-level countries to form an "extended" group:

Nigeria, Tanzania and Pakistan. Thus extended, the 21 countries constitute 53 per cent of the population of the developing world, and India forms 39 per cent of the total. The United Nations Population Division has been right to be cautious about overstating the speed of fertility decline. In comparison to other sources (DHS, INED, PRB), however, it seems now to be overstating the Bangladesh TFR, given as 3.6 in World Population 2000 and 3.7 by averaging the 1995-2000 estimate and 2000-2005 medium projection in the 2000 Review of Population Prospects.

A more probable estimate would seem to be around 3.3. Conversely, the TFRs of North Africa (Algeria, Egypt, Morocco, Sudan) appear to be understated, although less so in the averaged projections than in the World Population 2000 sheet. It might also be noted that some countries are difficult to treat as a single unit. In Nigeria the TFR in the relatively poor Muslim north is still around 7.0 while in the richer, more educated and predominately Christian south it is in the 4-5 range, comparable with Ghana and Kenya. Conversely, in Sudan it is the richer Muslim north that is characterised by lower fertility.

There no longer seem to be any barriers to most countries reaching replacement-level fertility and subsequently falling below that level; certainly not an income barrier, for Moldova and Armenia, with per capita purchasing power parity incomes (pci ppp) similar to that of India, exhibit TFRs of 1.4 and 1.1 respectively. Similarly, religious barriers are not insuperable, with fertility in Catholic Italy and Spain being little more than half replacement level, and in Muslim North Africa declining persistently. Threshold analysis has fallen into some disrepute, but low fertility levels are significantly correlated with high per capita incomes, low child mortality, high female educational and employment levels, and 77 urbanisation.

Employing such measures (pci ppp over US$2,000; under-five mortality below 75 per 1000 births; over 30 per cent of girls in secondary school; and over 40% urbanisation), 13 of the 21 countries examined here seem likely to exhibit below-replacement-level fertility well before 2050: a group in South America (Argentina, Brazil, Colombia and Mexico), another group in North Africa (Algeria, Egypt, Morocco), five Asian countries (Indonesia, Iran, Philippines, Turkey, Vietnam) and one in sub-Saharan Africa (South Africa).

Those less likely to do so by these criteria are Sudan, Nigeria, Kenya, Tanzania, Bangladesh, India, Pakistan and Myanmar. If another factor is added, government resolve in the form of an efficient family planning programme likely to be kept in place as fertility declines, then India, and possibly Bangladesh, could be transferred to the first group. Latin American fertility decline may have been retarded by the Catholic Church, as is evidenced by Argentina, which has a pci ppp around that of Hungary or the Czech Republic, but has been characterised by a TFR which over half a century from 1950 to 2000 fell only from 3.2 to 2.6.

Nevertheless, there may be a delayed parallel with the experience of Italy, Spain and Portugal, where TFRs were in the range 2.5-2.9 in 1965-1970, above those of Northern and Central Europe, but where now, at 1.1-1.5, they are below those of Northern Europe. Very low fertility may not even require employment for all women. Ever-higher levels of children's education, enforced by the principle of keeping up with the Joneses, may be enough. The foundation for fertility decline in Africa was laid by economic development, but subsequently the major force in reducing fertility seems to have been the costs of providing education and health care for children as African economies found themselves in trouble, and ensuing structural adjustment programmes imposed user pays fees for these services. Among the Indian urban elite single -child families are no longer rare.

Other factors may be more important, particularly the globalisation of markets and the consumer society, the aim of giving all girls a good education, and the belief that educated women should be employed outside the home. This has been given a new twist by the analysis of the factors determining Italy's very low fertility. It has been argued that many women cannot manage to stay successfully in the work force in a patriarchal society where husbands give little help with child care and other domestic work, and where the state does not intervene to help with preschool child care or employment provisions that do not penalise women for dropping out of the work force while they have young children.

It has also been argued that men are conditioned not to help in the household by their mothers during the long period of being in the parental house until marriage at, on average, almost 30 years of age. This has been compared with supposedly more helpful husbands in Northern Europe and the United States and more helpful governments in Northern and Central Europe. The irony of this comparison is that the Mediterranean patriarchal model is far more common in the world than the Northern European model and characterises Latin America, North Africa, sub-Saharan Africa, Western Asia, South Asia and East Asia. If the analyses of the Italian situation are correct, then below-replacement fertility may characterise most of the world by 2050.

My hunch about the 2000 Revision is that it is largely on the right track except for the medium projection bottoming so widely at a total fertility rate of 2.1 which is unlikely to prove the lower limit for the majority of countries. My interpretation of the evidence is that the caution about Bangladesh was justified but that it has now been somewhat overdone in terms of when replacement fertility will be reached.

POPULATION GROWTH: CHALLENGES AND OPPORTUNITIES

Human beings evolved under conditions of high mortality due to famines, accidents, illnesses, infections and war and therefore the relatively high fertility rates were essential for species survival. In spite of the relatively high fertility rates it took all the time from evolution of mankind to the middle of the 19th century for the global population to reach one billion. The twentieth century witnessed an unprecedented rapid improvement in health care technologies and access to health care all over the world; as a result there was a steep fall in the mortality and steep increase in longevity. The population realised these changes and took steps to reduce their fertility but the decline in fertility was not so steep. As a result the global population has undergone a fourfold increase in a hundred years and has reached 6 billion.

Demographic Transition

Demographers refer to these changes from stable population with high fertility and mortality to a new stability in population due to low fertility and mortality patterns as demographic transition. Demographic transition occurs in four phases; of these the first three phases are characterised by population growth. In the first phase there is a fall in death rate and improvement in longevity; this leads to population growth. In the second phase there is a fall in birth rate but fall is less steep than fall in death rates and consequently there is population growth.

In the third phase death rates plateau and replacement level of fertility is attained but the population growth continues because of the large size of population in reproductive age group. The fourth phase is characterised by fall in birth rate to below replacement level and reduction in the proportion of the population in reproductive age group; as a result of these changes population growth ceases and population stabilises. Experience in some of the developed countries suggest that in some societies even after attainment of stable population there may be a further decline in fertility so that there is a further reduction in the population- so called negative population growth phase of the demographic transition.

Different countries in the world have entered the demographic transition at different periods of time; there are also substantial differences in the rate of demographic transition and time taken to achieve population stabilisation.

Global Population Scenario

In 1901 the world population was 1.6 billion. By 1960, it became 3 billion, and by 1987, 5 billion and in 1999, 6 billion. Currently, one billion people are added every 12 - 13 years. During the last decade there has been substantial decline in birth rate. The reasons for decline vary from society to society; urbanisation, rising educational attainment, increasing employment among women, lower infant mortality are some major factors responsible for growing desire for smaller families; increasing awareness and improved access to contraception have made it possible for the majority of the couple to achieve the desired family size. In some countries slowing of the population growth has been due to an increase in mortality (e.g. HIV related mortality in sub-Saharan Africa).

As a result of all these the decline in the global population growth during the nineties is steeper than the earlier predictions. Currently, the annual increment is about 80 million. It is expected to decrease to about 64 million by 2020 -25 and to 33 million by 2045 -50; 95 % of the growth of population occurs in developing countries. Most demographers believe that the current accelerated decline in population growth will continue for the next few decades and the medium projections of Population Division of United Nations, that the global population will grow to 8.9 billion by 2050 is likely to be achieved.

Changing Age Structure of the Population

During demographic transition along with the growth in number there are changes in the population age structure. While the importance of the population growth as a determinant of quality of life is universally understood, the profoundly serious consequences of changing age structure especially if it occurs too rapidly is not understood by many. Population pyramids graphically represent complex changes in age structure of the population so that it can be readily understood and interpreted.

Currently nearly half of the global population is below 25 years of age and one sixth are in the age group 15-24. Their choices, efforts and lifestyles will determine not only the population growth but also future improvement in the quality of life in harmony with global ecology. In developed countries the reproductive age group population is relatively small; their fertility is low and the longevity at birth is high. Population profiles of these countries resemble a cylinder and not a pyramid.

These countries have the advantages of having achieved a stable population but have to face the problems of having a relatively small productive work force to support the large aged population with substantial non-communicable disease burden. Some of the developing countries have undergone a very rapid decline in the birth rates within a short period. This enabled them to quickly achieve population stabilisation but they do face the problems of rapid changes in the age structure and work force which may be inadequate to meet their manpower requirements.

In contrast the population in most of the developing countries (including India) consist of a very large proportion of children and persons in reproductive age. Because of the large reproductive age group (Population momentum) the population will continue to grow even when replacement level of fertility is reached (couples having only two children). It is imperative that these countries should generate enough employment opportunities for this work force and utilise the human resources and accelerate their economic growth. Planners and policy makers in developing countries like India have to take into account the ongoing demographic changes (number and age structure of the population) so that available human resources are optimal utilised as agents of change and development to achieve improvement in quality of life.

Demographic Transition in India

Over the last four decades there has been rapid fall in Crude

Death Rate (CDR) from 25.1 in 1951 to 9.8 in 1991 and less steep decline in the Crude Birth Rate (CBR) from 40.8 in 1951 to 29.5 in 1991. The annual exponential population growth rate has been over 2% in the period 1961-90. During the nineties the decline in CBR has been steeper than that in the (CDR) and consequently, the annual population growth rate has fallen below 2%.

The rate of decline in population growth is likely to be further accelerated during the next decade. The changes in the population growth rates have been relatively slow, steady and sustained. As a result the country was able to achieve a relatively gradual change in the population numbers and age structure. The short and long term adverse consequences of too rapid decline in birth rates and change in age structure on the social and economic development were avoided and the country was able to adapt to these changes without massive disruptions of developmental efforts. In spite of the uniform national norms set under the 100% Centrally Funded and Centrally Sponsored Scheme (CSS) of Family Welfare, there are substantial differences in the performance between States as assessed by IMR and CBR. Though the decline in CBR and IMR has occurred in all States, the rate of decline is slower in some States.

At one end of the spectrum is Kerala with mortality and fertility rates nearly similar to those in some of the developed countries. At the other end, there are four large northern States (Uttar Pradesh, Bihar, Madhya Pradesh and Rajasthan) with high Infant Mortality Rate and Fertility Rates. Though the decline in CBR, IMR and CDR has occurred in all States, the rate of decline was slower in some States like U.P. And Bihar. There are substantial differences in CBR and IMR not only between States but also between the districts in the same state.

In view of these findings, the NDC Committee on Population recommended that efforts should be made to provide reproductive and child health services at district level and undertake decentralised area-specific micro planning and implementation of appropriate interventions. In response to this recommendation Dept. of Family Welfare has abolished the practice of fixing targets for individual contraceptives by the Central Government from April 1996 and had initiated decentralised district based, planning (based on community need assessment), implementation, monitoring and mid-course corrections of FW programme. The experience of states with district based planning, implementation and the impact are being closely monitored.

Consequences of Population Growth

Environmental Consequences

In many developing countries continued population growth has resulted in pressure on land, fragmentation of land holding, collapsing fisheries, shrinking forests, rising temperatures, loss of plant and animal species. Global warming due to increasing use of fossil fuels (mainly by the developed countries) could have serious effects on the populous coastal regions in developing countries, their food production and essential water supplies. The Intergovernmental Panel on Climate Change has projected that, if current greenhouse gas emission trends continue, the mean global surface temperature will rise from 1 to 3.5 degrees Celsius in the next century.

The panel's best estimate scenario projects a sea-level rise of 15 to 95 centimetres by 2100. The ecological impact of rising oceans would include increased flooding, coastal erosion, salination of aquifers and coastal crop land and displacement of millions of people living near the coast. Patterns of precipitation are also likely to change, which combined with increased average temperatures, could substantially alter the relative agricultural productivity of different regions. Greenhouse gas emissions are closely linked to both population growth and development.

Slower population growth in developing countries and ecologically sustainable lifestyles in developed countries would make reduction in green house gas emission easier to achieve and provide more time and options for adaptation to climate change. Rapid population growth, developmental activities either to meet the growing population or the growing needs of the population as well as changing lifestyles and consumption patterns pose major challenge to preservation and promotion of ecological balance in India. Some of the major ecological adverse effects reported in India include:

- Severe pressure on the forests due to both the rate of resource use and the nature of use. The per capita forest bio-mass in the country is only about 6 tons as against the global average of 82 tons.
- Adverse effect on species diversity:
    - Conversion of habitat to some other land use such as agriculture, urban development, forestry operation. Some 70-80 % of fresh water marshes and lakes in the Gangetic flood plains has been lost in the last 50 years.
    - Tropical deforestation and destruction of mangroves for commercial needs and fuel wood. The country's mangrove areas have reduced from 700,000 ha to 453,000 ha in the last 50 years.
    - Intense grazing by domestic livestock
    - Poaching and illegal harvesting of wildlife.
    - Increase in agricultural area, high use of chemical fertilisers pesticides and we decides; water stagnation, soil erosion, soil salinity and low productivity.

— High level of bio-mass burning causing large-scale indoor pollution.

— Encroachment on habitat for rail and road construction thereby fragmenting the habitat. Increase in commercial activities such as mining and unsustainable resource extraction.

— Degradation of coastal and other aquatic ecosystems from domestic sewage, pesticides, fertilisers and industrial effluents.

— Over fishing in water bodies and introduction of weeds and exotic species.

— Diversion of water for domestic, industrial and agricultural uses leading to increased river pollution and decrease in self-cleaning properties of rivers.

— Increasing water requirement leading to tapping deeper aquifers which have high content of arsenic or fluoride resulting health problems.

— Disturbance from increased recreational activity and tourism causing pollution of natural ecosystems with wastes left behind by people.

The United Nations Conference on Environment and Development acknowledged population growth, rising income levels, changing technologies, increasing consumption pattern will all have adverse impact on environment. Ensuring that there is no further deterioration depends on choices made by the population about family size, life styles, environmental protection and equity. Availability of appropriate technology and commitment towards ensuring sustainable development is increasing throughout the world. Because of these, it might be possible to initiate steps to see that the natural carrying capacity of the environment is not damaged beyond recovery and ecological balance is to a large extent maintained. It is imperative that the environmental sustainability of all developmental projects is taken care of by appropriate inputs at the planning, implementation, monitoring and evaluation stages.

Urbanisation

The proportion of people in developing countries who live in cities has almost doubled since 1960 (from less than 22 per cent to more than 40 per cent), while in more developed regions the urban share has grown from 61 per cent to 76 per cent. Urbanisation is projected to continue well into the next century. By 2030, it is expected that nearly 5 billion (61 per cent) of the world's 8.1 billion people will live in cities. India shares this global trend toward urbanisation.

Globally, the number of cities with 10 million or more inhabitants is increasing rapidly, and most of these new "megacities" are in developing regions. In 1960, only New York and Tokyo had more than 10 million people. By 1999, the number of megacities had grown to 17(13 in developing countries). It is projected that there will be 26 megacities by 2015, (18 in Asia; of these five in India); more than 10 per cent of the world's population will live in these cities. India's urban population has doubled from 109 million to 218 million during the last two decades and is estimated to reach 300 million by 2000 AD. As a consequence cities are facing the problem of expanding urban slums.

Like many other demographic changes, urbanisation has both positive and negative effects. Cities and towns have become the engines of social change and rapid economic development. Urbanisation is associated with improved access to education, employment, health care; these result in increase in age at marriage, reduction in family size and improvement in health indices. As people have moved towards and into cities, information has flowed outward.

Better communication and transportation now link urban and rural areas both economically and socially creating an urban-rural continuum of communities with improvement in some aspects of lifestyle of both.

The ever increasing reach of mass media communicate new ideas, points of reference, and available options are becoming more widely recognised, appreciated and sought. This phenomenon has affected health care, including reproductive health, in many ways. For instance, radio and television programmes that discuss gender equity, family size preference and family planning options are now reaching formerly isolated rural populations. This can create demand for services for mothers and children, higher contraceptive use, and fewer unwanted pregnancies, smaller healthier families and lead to more rapid population stabilisation.

But the rapid growth of urban population also poses some serious challenges. Urban population growth has outpost the development of basic minimum services; housing, water supply, sewerage and solid waste disposal are far from adequate; increasing waste generation at home, offices and industries, coupled with poor waste disposal facilities result in rapid environmental deterioration. Increasing automobiles add to air pollution. All these have adverse effect on ecology and health. Poverty persists in urban and peri-urban areas; awareness about the glaring inequities in close urban setting may lead to social unrest.

Rural Population and their Development

Over seventy per cent of India's population still lives in rural areas. There are substantial differences between the states in the proportion of rural and urban population (varying from almost 90 per cent in Assam and Bihar to 61 per cent in Maharashtra). Agriculture is the largest and one of the most important sector of the rural economy and contributes both to economic growth and employment. Its contribution to the Gross Domestic Product has declined over the last five decades but agriculture still remains the source of livelihood for over 70 per cent of the country's population. A large proportion of the rural work force is small and consists of marginal farmers and landless agricultural labourers. There is substantial under employment among these people; both wages and productivity are low. These in turn result in poverty; it is estimated that 320 million people are still living below the poverty line in rural India.

Though poverty has declined over the last three decades, the number of rural poor has in fact increased due to the population growth. Poor tend to have larger families which puts enormous burden on their meagre resources, and prevent them from breaking out of the shackles of poverty. In States like Tamil Nadu where replacement level of fertility has been attained, population growth rates are much lower than in many other States; but the population density is high and so there is a pressure on land. In States like Rajasthan, Uttar Pradesh, Bihar and Madhya Pradesh population is growing rapidly, resulting in increasing pressure on land and resulting land fragmentation.

Low productivity of small land holders leads to poverty, low energy intake and under nutrition, and this, in turn, prevents the development thus creating a vicious circle. In most of the states non-farm employment in rural areas has not grown very much and cannot absorb the growing labour force. Those who are getting educated specially beyond the primary level, may not wish to do manual agricultural work. They would like better opportunities and more remunerative employment. In this context, it is imperative that programmes for skill development, vocational training and technical education are taken up on a large scale in order to generate productive employment in rural areas. The entire gamut of existing poverty alleviation and employment generation programmes may have to be restructured to meet the newly emerging types of demand for employment.

Rural poor have inadequate access to basic minimum services, because of poor connectivity, lack of awareness, inadequate and poorly functional infrastructure. There are ongoing efforts to improve these, but with the growing aspirations of the younger, educated population these efforts may prove to be inadequate to meet the increasing needs both in terms of type and quality of services.

Greater education, awareness and better standard of living among the growing younger age group population would create the required consciousness among them that smaller families are desirable; if all the felt needs for health and family welfare services are fully met, it will be possible to enable them to attain their reproductive goals, achieve substantial decline in the family size and improve quality of life.

Water Supply

In many parts of developed and developing world, water demand substantially exceeds sustainable water supply. It is estimated that currently 430 millions (8% of the global population) are living in countries affected by water stress; by 2020 about one fourth of the global population may be facing chronic and recurring shortage of fresh water. In India, water withdrawal is estimated to be twice the rate of aquifer recharge; as a result water tables are falling by one to three meters every year; tapping deeper aquifers have resulted in larger population groups being exposed to newer health hazards such as high fluoride or arsenic content in drinking water.

At the other end of the spectrum, excessive use of water has led to water logging and increasing salinity in some parts of the country. Eventually, both lack of water and water logging could have adverse impact on India's food production. There is very little arable agricultural land which remains un exploited and in many areas, agricultural technology improvement may not be able to ensure further increase in yield per hectare. It is, therefore, imperative that research in biotechnology for improving development of food grains strains that would tolerate salinity and those which would require less water gets high priority. Simultaneously, a movement towards making water harvesting, storage and its need based use part of every citizens life should be taken up.

Food Security

Technological innovations in agriculture and increase in area under cultivation have ensured that so far, food production has kept pace with the population growth. Evolution of global and national food security systems have improved access to food. It is estimated that the global population will grow to 9 billion by 2050 and the food production will double; improvement in purchasing power and changing dietary habits (shift to animal products) may further add to the requirement of food grains. Thus, in the next five decades, the food and nutrition security could become critical in many parts of the world especially in the developing countries and pockets of poverty in the developed countries.

In India one of the major achievements in the last fifty years has been the green revolution and self-sufficiency in food production. Food grain production has increased from 50.82 in 1950-51 to 200.88 million tons in 1998-99.

It is a matter of concern that while the cereal production has been growing steadily at a rate higher than the population growth rates, the coarse grain and pulse production has not shown a similar increase. Consequently there has been a reduction in the per capita availability of pulses and coarse grains.

Over the last five decades there has been a decline in the per capita availability of pulses. During the last few years the country has imported pulses to meet the requirement. There has been a sharp and sustained increase in cost of pulses, so there is substantial decline in per capita pulses consumption among poorer segment of population. This in turn could have an adverse impact on their protein intake. The pulse component of the "Pulses and Oil Seeds Mission" need to receive a major thrust in terms of R&D and other inputs, so that essential pulse requirement of growing population is fully met. Rising cost of pulses had a beneficial effect also. Till eighties in central India wages of landless labourers were given in the form Kesari Dal which was cheaper than cereals or coarse grains. Consumption of staple diet of Kesari Dal led to crippling disease of neuro lathyrism. Over the last three decades the rising cost of pulses has made Kesari Dal more expensive than wheat or rice and hence it is no longer given to labourers as wages for work done; as a result the disease has virtually disappeared from Central India.

Over years the coarse grain production has remained stagnant and per capita availability of coarse grain has under gone substantial reduction; there has been a shift away from coarse grains to rice and wheat consumption even among poorer segment of population. One of the benefits of this change is virtual elimination of pellagra which was widely prevalent among low income group population in Deacon Plateau whose staple food was sorghum.

Coarse grains are less expensive than rice and wheat; they can thus provide higher calories for the same cost as compared to rice and wheat. Coarse grains which are locally produced and procured if made available through TPDS at subsidised rate, may not only substantially bring down the subsidy cost without any reduction in calories provided but also improve "targeting"—as only the most needy are likely to access these coarse grains.

Another area of concern is the lack of sufficient focus and thrust in horticulture; because of this, availability of vegetables especially green leafy vegetables and yellow/red vegetables throughout the year at affordable cost both in urban and rural areas has remained an unfulfilled dream. Health and nutrition education emphasising the importance of consuming these inexpensive rich sources of micro-nutrients will not result in any change in food habits unless there is harnessing and effective management of horticultural resources in the country to meet the growing needs of the people at affordable cost. States like Tamil Nadu and Himachal Pradesh have initiated some efforts in this direction; similar efforts need be taken up in other states also.

Nutrition

At the time of independence the country faced two major nutritional problems; one was the threat of famine and acute starvation due to low agricultural production and lack of appropriate food distribution system. The other was chronic energy deficiency due to poverty, low-literacy, poor access to safe-drinking water, sanitation and health care; these factors led to wide spread prevalence of infections and ill health in children and adults. Kwashiorkor, marasmus, goitre, berry, blindness due to Vitamin-A deficiency and anaemia were major public health problems.

The country adopted multi-sectorial, multi-pronged strategy to combat the major nutritional problems and to improve nutritional status of the population. During the last 50 years considerable progress has been achieved. Famines no longer stalk the country. There has been substantial reduction in moderate and severe undernutrition in children and some improvement in nutritional status of all segments of population. Kwashiorkor, marasmus, pellagra, lathyrism, berry and blindness due to severe Vitamin-A deficiency have become rare.

However, it is a matter of concern that milder forms of Chronic Energy Deficiency (CED) and micronutrient deficiencies continue to be widely prevalent in adults and children. In view of the fact that population growth in India will continue for the next few decades, it is essential that appropriate strategies are devised to improve food and nutrition security of families, identify individuals/families with severe forms of CED and provide them assistance to over come these problem. Operational strategy to improve the dietary intake of the family and improve nutritional status of the rapidly growing adult population would include:

— Ensuring adequate agricultural production of cereals, pulses, vegetables and other foodstuffs needed to fully meet the requirement of growing population.

— Improving in purchasing power through employment generation and employment assurance schemes.

— Providing subsidised food grains through TPDS to the families below poverty line.

— Exploring feasibility of providing subsidised coarse grains to families Below Poverty Line (BPL).

Operational strategies to improve health and nutritional status of the growing numbers of women and children include:

— *Pregnant and lactating women*: screening to identify women with weight below 40 Kg and ensuring that they/ their preschool children receive food supplements through Integrated Child Development Services Scheme (ICDS); adequate antenatal intrapartum and neonatal care.

— *0-6 months infants:* Nutrition education for:
  — Early initiation of lactation.
  — Protection and promotion of universal breast feeding.
  — Exclusive breast feeding for the first six months; unless there is specific reason supplementation should not be introduced before 6 months.
  — Immunisation, growth monitoring and health care.

— Well planned nutrition education to ensure that the infants and children do:
  — Continue to get breasted.
  — *Get appropriate cereal pulse:* vegetable based supplement fed to them at least 3 - 4 times a day – appropriate help in ensuring this through family/community/work place support.
  — Immunisation and health care.

— *Children in the 0:* 5 age group:
  — Screen by weighment to identify children with moderate and severe undernutrition.
  — Provide double quantity supplements through ICDS.
  — Screening for nutrition and health problems and appropriate intervention.

— *Primary school children:*
  — Weigh and identify those with moderate and severe chronic energy deficiency.
  — Improve dietary intake to these children through the midday meal.

— Monitor for improvement in the identified undernourished infants, children and mothers; if no improvement after 2 months refer to physician for identification and treatment of factors that might be responsible for lack of improvement.

— Nutrition education on varying dietary needs of different members of the family and how they can be met by minor modifications from the family meals. Intensive health education for improving the life style of the population coupled with active screening and management of the health problems associated with obesity.

Population Projections and their Implications

Right from 1958 the Planning Commission has been constituting an Expert Group on Population Projections prior to the preparation of each of the Five Year Plans so that the information on the population status at the time of initiation of the Plan and population projections for future are available during the preparation of the Plan. Population projections have been utilised not only for planning to ensure provision of essentials necessities such as food, shelter and clothing but also prerequisites for human development such as education, employment and health care. Over the years there has been considerable refinement in the methodology used for population projections and substantial improvement in the accuracy of predictions. The projections made by the Standing Committee on Population Projection in 1988 for the year 1991 was 843.6 million; this figure was within 0.3% of the 846.3 million reported in the Census 1991. In 1996, Technical Group on Population Projections, had work out the population projections for the country and the states for the period 1996 to 2016 on the basis of census 1991 and other available demographic data.

Economic Implications

Population growth and its relation to economic growth has been a matter of debate for over a century. The early

Malthusian view was that population growth is likely to impede economic growth because it will put pressure on the available resources, result in reduction in per capita income and resources; this, in turn, will result in deterioration in quality of life. Contrary to the Malthusian predictions, several of the East Asian countries have been able to achieve economic prosperity and improvement in quality of life inspite of population growth. This has been attributed to the increase in productivity due to development and utilisation of innovative technologies by the young educated population who formed the majority of the growing population. These countries have been able to exploit the dynamics of demographic transition to achieve economic growth by using the human resources as the engine driving the economic development; improved employment with adequate emoluments has promoted saving and investment which in turn stimulated economic growth.

However, not all countries, which have undergone demographic transition, have been able to transform their economies. Sri Lanka in South Asia underwent demographic transition at the same time as South East Asian countries but has not achieved the economic transition. It is now realised that population growth or demographic transition can have favourable impact on economic growth only when there are optimal interventions aimed at human resource development (HRD) and appropriate utilisation of available human resources.

For India the current phase of demographic transition with low dependency ratio and high working age group population, represents both a challenge and an opportunity. The challenge is to develop these human resources through appropriate education and skill development and utilise them fully by giving them appropriate jobs with adequate emoluments; if this challenge is met through well planned schemes for HRD and employment generation which are implemented effectively, there will be improved national productivity and personal savings rates; appropriate investment of these savings will help the country to achieve the economic transition from low economic growth - low per capita income to high economic growth - high per capita income. It is imperative to make the best use of this opportunity so as to enable the country and its citizens to vault to the high income- high economic growth status and stabilise at that level.

Interstate Differences

There are marked differences between States in size of the population and population growth rates, the time by which replacement level of fertility is to be achieved and age structure of the population. If the present trend continues, most of the Southern and the Western States are likely to achieve TFR of 2.1 by 2010. Urgent energetic steps to assess and fully meet the unmet needs for maternal and child health (MCH) care and contraception through improvement in availability and access to family welfare services are needed in the States of UP, MP, Rajasthan and Bihar in order to achieve a faster decline in their mortality and fertility rates.

The five states of Bihar, Uttar Pradesh, Madhya Pradesh, Rajasthan and Orissa, which constitute 44% of the total population of India in 1996, will constitute 48% of the total population of India in 2016. These states will contribute 55% of the total increase in population of the country during the period 1996-2016. In all the states performance in the social and economic sector has been poor. The poor performance is the outcome of poverty, illiteracy and poor development which coexist and reinforce each other.

The quality and coverage under health services is poor and the unmet need for FW services is about 30%. Urgent energetic steps are required to be initiated to assess and fully meet the unmet needs for maternal and child health (MCH) care and contraception through improvement in availability and access to family welfare services in the states of UP, MP, Rajasthan and Bihar in order to achieve a faster decline in their mortality and fertility rates. The performance of these states would determine the year and size of the population at which the country achieves population stabilisation.

There are also marked differences between States in socioeconomic development. Increasing investments and rapid economic development are likely to occur in the States where literacy rates are high; there is ready availability of skilled work force and adequate infrastructure. In these States, population growth rates are low. If equitable distribution of the income and benefits generated by development is ensured, substantial increase in per capita income and improvement in quality of life could occur in these States in a relatively short time.

In majority of States with high population growth rates, the performance in the social and economic sector has been poor. The poor performance could be the outcome of a variety of factors including paucity of natural, financial or human resources. Poverty, illiteracy and poor development coexist and aggravate each other. In order to promote equity and reduce disparity between States, special assistance has been provided to the poorly performing States. The benefits accrued from such assistance has to a large extent depended upon:

- The States' ability to utilise the available funds; improve quality & coverage of services and facilities, increase efficiency and improve performance.
- Community awareness and ability to utilise the available services.

- — In spite of the additional assistance provided, improvement in infrastructure, agriculture and industry have been suboptimal and the per capita income continues to be low in most of the poorly performing States.
- — These States also have high birth rates and relatively low literacy rates. It is imperative that special efforts are made during the next two decades to break this vicious self perpetuating cycle of poor performance, poor per capita income, poverty, low literacy and high birth rate so that the further widening of disparities between States in terms of per capita income and quality of life is prevented.

The higher population growth rates and low per capita income in poorly performing States are likely to have a major impact on several social sector programmes. The health status of the population in these States is poor; the health sector programme will require inputs not only for improving infrastructure and manpower, but also increasing efficiency and improving performance. The Family Welfare Programme has to address the massive task of meeting all the unmet needs for MCH and contraception so that there is a rapid decline in mortality and fertility rates. Due to high birth rate, the number of children requiring schooling will be large.

The emphasis in the education sector on primary education is essential to ensure that the resource constraints do not result in an increase in either proportion or number of illiterates. Emphasis on pre-vocational and vocational training in schools will enable these children to acquire skills through which they will find gainful employment later.

Migration

The available data from census shows that until 1991 both

internal and international migration has been negligible. The Technical Group while computing the population projection up to 2016, has assumed that the component of migration between major States and from India will be negligible. This assumption may not be valid if there is further widening of the disparity between States in terms of economic growth and employment opportunity.

Given the combination of high population growth, low literacy and lack of employment opportunities in the poorly performing States, there may be increasing rural to urban migration as well as interstate migration especially of unskilled workers. Such migration may in the short run assist the migrants in overcoming economic problems associated with unemployment. However, the migrant workers and their families may face problems in securing shelter, education and health care. It is essential to build up a mechanism for monitoring these changes. Steps will have to be taken to provide for the minimum essential needs of the vulnerable migrant population.

Labour, Employment and Manpower

Population, which is engaged in any economic activity (employed persons) and population seeking work (unemployed) constitute Labour Force. India has the second largest labour force in the world. Projection of labour force is prerequisite ensuring optimal utilisation of available human resources. Manpower development is then taken up to provide adequate labour force, of appropriate skills and quality to different sectors so that there is rapid socioeconomic development and there is no mismatch between skills required and skills available. Planning also attempts to provide enabling environment for employment generation (both self employment and wage employment) in public, private and voluntary sectors in urban and rural areas.

Labour force in India will be increasing by more than 10 million per annum during 1997-2012. It will be imperative to plan for and achieve adequate agricultural and industrial growth to absorb this work force. Most of the persons entering the labour force will be educated and have some skills. Increasing literacy and decreasing birth rates may result in more women seeking economically productive work outside home. It will be important to generate appropriate and re-numerative employment at places where labour force are available so as to reduce interstate and urban migration in search of employment. Attempts should be made to eliminate bonded labour, employment of children and women in hazardous industries and minimising occupational health hazards.

Planners face the challenge to have sustained high economic growth rate in sectors that are labour-intensive to ensure adequate employment generation for productively utilising this massive work force. If the massive work force of literate, skilled, aware men and women in age-group 20-60 years get fully employed and adequately paid they could trigger off a period of rapid economic development. As they have very few dependant children and elders there will be increased savings and investments at household level; this in turn will improve the availability of resources for accelerating economic growth. The current stage of demographic transition thus provides the country with the opportunity window for using human resources as the engine to power economic development and improving the quality of life of all the citizens.

Sex Ratio

The reported decline in the sex ratio during the current century has been a cause for concern. The factors responsible for this continued decline are as yet not clearly identified. However, it is well recognised that the adverse sex ratio is a reflection of the gender disparity. Higher childhood mortality in girl children is yet another facet of the existing gender disparities and consequent adverse effect on survival.

In the reproductive age group the mortality rates among women are higher than those among men. The continued high maternal mortality is one of the major factors responsible for this. Effective implementation of the Reproductive and Child Health Programme is expected to result in a substantial reduction in maternal mortality. At the moment, the longevity at birth among women is only marginally higher than that among men. However over the next decade life expectancy among women will progressively increase. Once the reproductive age group is crossed, the mortality rates among women are lower as women outlive and outnumber men in the age group 65 and above. The needs especially of the widowed women have to be met so that quality of life does not deteriorate.

The census 2001 will collect and report vital data on sex disaggregated basis; this will be of help in identifying and taking up appropriate interventions in correcting gender disparity; continued collection, collation, analysis and reporting of sex disaggregated data from all social sectors will also provide a mechanism to monitor whether girls and women have equal access to services.

Increasing Longevity

Over the coming decades the country will be facing a progressive increase both in the proportion and number of persons beyond 60 years of age. Over the next 20 years the population of more than 60 years will grow form 62.3 million to 112.9 million; the subsequent decades will witness massive increase in this age group. Increasing longevity will inevitably bring in its wake increase in the prevalence of non-communicable diseases.

The growing number of senior citizens in the country poses a major challenge and the cost of providing socioeconomic security and health care to this population has to be met. Currently several region and culture specific innovative interventions to provide needed care to this population are underway; among these are efforts to reverse the trend of break up of joint families. If these efforts succeed, it will be possible to provide necessary care for rapidly increasing population of senior citizens in the subsequent two decades within the resources of the family and the country.

Majority of the people in their sixties will be physically and psychologically fit and would like to participate both in economic and social activities. They should be encouraged and supported to lead a productive life and contribute to the national development. Senior citizens in their seventies and beyond and those with health problems would require assistance. So far, the families have borne major share in caring for the elderly. This will remain the ideal method; however, there are growing number of elderly without family support; for them, alternate modes for caring may have to be evolved and implemented. Improved health care has "added years to life". The social sectors have to make the necessary provisions for improving the quality of life of these senior citizens so that they truly " add life to years."

Health Implication of Demographic Transition

It was earlier assumed that population growth during demographic transition will lead to overcrowding, poverty, undernutrition, environmental deterioration, poor quality of life and increase in disease burden. Experience in the last few decades have shown that this may not always be correct. India is currently in the phase of demographic transition when the increase in population is mainly among younger, better educated and healthy population with low morbidity and mortality rate. The challenge for the health sector is to promote healthy life styles, improve access to and utilisation of health care so that the country can achieve substantial reduction in mortality and morbidity.

Occupational health and environmental health programme need be augmented to ensure that working population remain healthy and productive. If these challenges are fully met, it is possible to accelerate reduction in morbidity and mortality rate in this age group and improve health indices of the country.

With growing number of senior citizens there may be substantial increase in health care needs especially for management of non-communicable diseases. Increasing availability and awareness about technological advances for management of these problems, rising expectations of the population and the ever escalating cost of health care are some of the problems that the health care system has to cope with. Health care delivery systems will have to gear up to taking up necessary preventive, promotive, curative and rehabilitative care for growing population of senior citizens.

Implications on FW Programme

There will be a marginal decline in the population less than 15 years of age (352.7 million to 350.4 million). The health care infrastructure will therefore be not grappling with ever increasing number of children for providing care and they will be able to concentrate on: a. Improving quality of care; b. focus on antenatal, intranatal and neonatal care aimed at reducing neonatal morbidity and mortality; c. Improve coverage and quality of health care to vulnerable and under served adolescents; d. promote inter sectorial coordination especially with ICDS programme so that there is improvement in health and nutritional status; e. Improve coverage for immunisation against vaccine preventable diseases. The economic challenge is to provide needed funds so that these children have access to nutrition, education and skill development. The challenge faced by the health sector is to achieve reduction in morbidity and mortality rate in infancy and childhood, to improve nutritional status and eliminate ill-effects of gender bias.

There will be a massive increase of population in the 15-59 age group (from 519 million to 800 million). The persons in this age group will be more literate and have greater access to information; they will therefore have greater awareness and expectation regarding both the access to a wide spectrum of health care related services and the quality of these services. Under the Reproductive and child health care programme efforts are underway to provide:

— Needed services for this rapid growing population
— To broaden the spectrum of services available and
— To improve quality and coverage of health care to women, children and adolescents, so that their felt needs for health care are fully met.
— To improve the participation of men in the planned parenthood movement.

While providing the package of services, efforts will have to be made to improve the quality of services, make services more responsive to users' needs, ensure that health workers and health care providers have the necessary skills and supplies they need and there is a strong and effective referral system to manage all the risk cases. Family welfare Programme is attempting to improve the logistics of supply of drugs and vaccine to make sure good quality drugs are available at appropriate time.

Simultaneously the IEC efforts are being directed to:

— Ensure responsible reproductive /sexual behaviour.
— Improve awareness about reproductive health needs.

— Promote community participation and optimal utilisation of available services.

— Essential Reproductive and Child Health Services.

Though it is desirable that the entire package of services indicated under comprehensive RCH care is made available to all those who need it, will not be possible to immediately implement such a comprehensive package at primary health care level on a nationwide basis. After consultation with experts a package of essential reproductive health services for nationwide implementation at primary health care settings has been identified. Essential components recommended for nationwide implementation include:

— Prevention and management of unwanted pregnancy.

— Services to provide antenatal, intranatal and postnatal, and neonatal care.

— Services to promote child health and survival.

— Prevention and treatment of RTI/STD.

Most of these services are already being delivered under the Family Welfare Programme. However, there are wide variations in the quality and coverage of services not only between states but also between districts in the same state. The focus under RCH Programme is therefore on the improvement in the quality and coverage of the services over and above the existing level in all districts/states in an incremental manner so that there is over all improvement maternal and child health indices.

10

Threats of Terrorism

The subject of "terrorism" seized the world's attention in late as a result of one fairly brief, yet highly dramatic and destructive, attack on two of the core symbols of the world's most powerful political actor, the United States of America. The targeting of the World Trade Center in New York City, the symbol of the United States' enormous global economic power, and the Pentagon Building in Washington, DC, the symbol of the United States' overarching military superiority, was well planned, coordinated, and executed. The attack itself attained symbolic stature as an affront to the established global order, a challenge to the world's dominant power, and an announcement that the prevailing US-led global order was not viewed, or valued, equally by all those whose daily lives are increasingly caught in the vortex of post-Cold War change.

Of course, the problem of terrorism was already well-known when the planes struck their targets in full view of a vast, global, tele-connected audience and created their indelible psychic images of sophisticated savagery. The politics of terror, and the overpowering fear that terror produces in its wake, lay at the very foundation of the evolution of social order. And it is the ultimate irony of societal development that modern acts of savagery have attained such high levels of sophistication. In its most simple terms, terror has stood as the stark alternative to civility in social relations from the time of humankind's earliest recorded reflections.

Analysing the Problem of Terrorism

Contemporary analyses of the problem of terrorism have usually foundered between the perceptual extremes that are inherent in the amorphous ideas of terror: conceptualizations of terrorism are either too broad to be analytically useful, too narrow to be analytically meaningful, or too complex to be applied systematically. The conceptualizations themselves are all too often politically motivated as the analyst attempts to rationalize a distinction between civil and uncivil applications of violence: (useless) terror and (useful) enforcement, (undisciplined) terrorism and (disciplined) war, and (dishonorable) terrorists and (honorable) "freedom fighters." Conceptual confusion is further exacerbated by the often cavalier usage of the pejorative term "terrorist" to refer to any political opponent, much as "communist" was used for political effect in the West during the Cold War.

Hoffman offers an example of a broad definition, "[Terrorism is] the deliberate creation and exploitation of fear through violence or the threat of violence in the pursuit of political change." Hoffman attempts to differentiate his definition of terrorism from criminal and lunatic violence by emphasizing the "altruistic" and "intellectual" qualities of terrorist motivation. However, it seems clear that all acts of terrorism are criminalized acts that are made particularly effective because they are unconventional (extralegal or non-rational) applications of violent or coercive behavior.

The parallels between terrorism, state repression, organized crime, and war are too great to be discounted. The use of arbitrary and indiscriminate violence in wartime has become increasingly criminalized since the establishment of the Nuremberg trials at the end of the Second World War in . State repression, or "state terror," which finds its most extreme form in totalitarianism has become increasingly scrutinized and criminalized by the international community. In a similarly broad definition, Carr goes so far as to equate terrorism with conventional warfare, with one very important distinction: "Terrorism is warfare deliberately waged against civilians with the purpose of destroying their will to support either leaders or policies that the agents of such violence find objectionable."

For Carr, terror is established through the unrestrained demonstration of violence; it is an induced emotional state intended to disable the will in individuals to resist, or seek rectification for, a perceived injustice through the credible threat (fear) of unspecified, unbearable consequences. While both Hoffman and Carr concentrate on the serious psycho-social affects of terror, their perspectives are separated widely by the perquisites of power: Hoffman's low-power, non-state terrorists using terror to challenge authority and facilitate change, Carr's high-power, state terrorists using terror to establish authority and facilitate conquest.

Schmid and Jongman provide an example of a definition of terrorism which, due ironically to their attempt to increase definitional specificity, is far too complex (and, at once, too broad) to be applied systematically in research. For them, terrorism is

> [a]n anxiety-inspiring method of repeated violent action, employed by (semi-) clandestine individual, group, or state actors, for idiosyncratic, criminal or political reasons, whereby – in contrast to assassination – the direct targets of violence are not the main targets. The immediate human victims of violence are generally chosen randomly (targets of opportunity) or selectively (representative or symbolic targets) from a target population, and serve as message generators. Threat- and violence-based communication processes between terrorist (organizations), (imperilled)

> victims, and main targets are used to manipulate the main target (audience(s)), turning it into a target of terror, a target of demands, or a target of attention, depending on whether intimidation, coercion, or propaganda is primarily used

The core qualities of Schmid and Jongman's definition are its inclusion of state actors, as well as non-state actors, as potential agents; its inclusion of wide ranges of power and political intent, and its recognition that acts of violence must be reiterative and somewhat arbitrary in order to induce widespread terror (rather than the more immediate response of revulsion to acts of brutality). Pillar emphasizes this later point in his definition of terrorism, that terror gains its greatest strength from its focus on the possible future rather than the knowable present.

A variant of the "narrow" approach to defining the problem of terrorism has been to identify a special class of terrorist activity, that is, "international," or "transnational," terrorism.8 This conceptualization has gained currency among policy-makers, particularly in "global powers" of the West, as it appears, on surface, to focus on a particular subset of terrorist actions with "global scope," thereby inferring that this subset of terrorism stands as a direct threat to the "global social order.

The concept is based on two important, implicit, a priori assumptions: first, the West, and particularly the US, is the recognized authority leading the establishment of an emerging global order and, second, the actions taken by the leading authorities in establishing and maintaining the emerging global order are either legitimate by definition (an extended form of the classic raison d'état) or that the interests of populations affected by the global order are adequately represented within the emerging global political system. This narrow form of terrorism, then, is conducted by those, usually non-state actors who may or may not receive support from dissident states or populations, who are intent on challenging, and changing, the terms of the prevailing social order. The essential qualities of this conceptualization relate to issues of distance and jurisdiction.

The first quality, distance or "reach," may be best viewed as simply a spatial artifact, often made salient by asymmetries of power between contending groups and established authorities. That is, challengers to a particular form of social order take advantage of available technologies and the prevailing vulnerabilities associated with distance by using, or seeking to exploit, available advantages in communication, information, and mobility to identify and attack relatively distant (and comparatively weak) outposts of authority. This spatial component of international terrorism is not unique, however. Opposition always operates near the boundaries of the collective consciousness as it is shaped by central authorities. Most acts of non-international terrorism have similar qualities of combining local, proximate, and distant action. In a strategic interaction between distanced groups, what is considered local to one is necessarily considered distant by the other. Agents of violence find it logistically easier to conduct local attacks but strategically important to demonstrate their capability to mount attacks on relationally distant targets located in their opponent's heartland. The perceived value, and therefore the terror potential, of targets increase with proximity to the heartland (and breach of the security perimeter).

Two contending groups rarely occupy the exact same political space and, even when they do share competing claims to authority over the same political space, their "heartlands" remain spatially distinct and separated even when their territorial or jurisdictional interests contend and overlap. So, for instance, the Irish Republican Army has operated mainly in the British province of Northern Ireland but has conducted operations in London at the center of the British heartland; the Tamils of Sri Lanka have struck targets both in Colombo (the Sinhalese heartland) and in India, including the May assassination of Indian Prime Minister Rajiv Gandhi; and Chechen militants have allegedly struck targets as "remote" as Moscow.

The relatively recent "internationalization" of anti-authority terrorism may be simply a function of increased popular access to distance or technological reach. Friedman has referred to this phenomenon as the "super-empowered individual." Such strategic behavior is not confined to asymmetric power relationships or non-state actors. The US air raids against Tokyo in April and NATO air raids against Belgrade during the Kosovo war are similar demonstrations of the capability to mount "distant" attacks in the opposition's heartland.

The second essential quality of international terrorism, jurisdiction, is particularly important in defining potential remedies to a contestation between groups or individuals. Operating outside of, or across, an established juridical boundary complicates remedial action (ameliorative or coercive) and limits the range and/or effectiveness of institutional options. With the lack of definitive and effective instruments for addressing the problem of terrorist action in international law and institutions, ambiguities and uncertainties of juridical responsibility provide special opportunities and vulnerabilities for exploitation both by terrorist agents and affected authorities.

In the absence of established institutional mechanisms, it can be expected that those entities that are most greatly affected and who enjoy the greatest capacity for direct action will act within such a "political vacuum" in terms of their own perspectives and according to their own interests, that is, unilaterally. The unregulated strategic interactions of the most directly affected parties played out in the greater communal space will undoubtedly serve to terrorize the entire system, creating a global imperative to act. But the ability to respond rationally and effectively will be limited by selection biases inherent in our understandings of the problem.

Again, selection biases often reflect asymmetries of power. Powerful actors have recourse to a wide array of instrumentalities to promote their parochial interests, whereas weak actors may feel they have very few options to demonstrate their position and the strength of their resolve other than violence. Diffuse and indirect actions often have very direct consequences, as Galtung has argued with his concept of "structural violence." Such structural violence, that is, violence embedded in the underlying structures of social relationships, is necessarily biased toward power and established authority and, thus, makes it particularly difficult to identify the interactive, reciprocal, and alternating qualities of "terrorist" and "terrorized."

The problems of distance and jurisdiction act within a context of immediacy and imperative created by the violent attack and, as such, treatments of the problem of international terrorism tend to favor emotive and reactive responses, focusing on the symptoms and rarely considering the nature of the problems that might have stimulated such extreme or radical actions. While studies of international terrorism usually contain the recognition of the political intent of terrorist acts, the convention of non-negotiation with terrorists often obviates the identification of possible motives and, thus, stifles our ability to avoid or preclude the resort to terrorism (which would, of course, obviate the need to negotiate with terrorists).

In addition to ignoring the structural foundations of terrorism, the literature on international terrorism does not usually include reference to comparable attacks on agents and institutions of international organizations such as the UN, international NGOs, and international journalists, thus confounding that concept with "anti-internationalist" or "anti-US" resistance. This is especially confusing in a global environment where the vestiges of "anti-colonialism" often intertwine with emerging strands of "anti-globalism." In systematic studies of international terrorism, the US, Israel, and the former colonial powers of Western Europe account for the vast majority of the targets of international terrorist acts.

The fact that the US, especially, enjoys an unprecedented extent of "international reach" in global affairs and, therefore, runs an unprecedented level of risk from engendered international contention should not be conflated with, and used as, a measure of the general security of the global system. In this sense, both the United States' proactive policies and reactions to those policies must be included in any objective measure of the affects of such strategic interaction on global security.

Perhaps the most difficult aspect to reconcile in our various attempts to define terrorism has been the almost universal claim that terrorism is necessarily political. Beyond the broadest sense of what is political, that is, the sense in which all actions taken in a social context are inherently political, the idea that an action is political implies that the action is instrumental in pursuing or achieving some commonly understood goal. On surface, action in pursuit of a goal must be considered rational, however, when the evidence strongly suggests that such action is largely ineffective in attaining the desired goals, the action, or strategy, must be considered irrational in practice. This is the "lesson" that Carr argues in The Lessons of Terror, that is, that terror is not rational; it is, rather, counter-productive to the general pursuit of political goals.

This is the central argument in my earlier examination of the problem of violence in the context of societal and systemic development. This rationality conundrum presents terrorism as an unsolvable problem. The conundrum can only be reconciled by examining the emotive qualities of terrorism: that terrorism is borne of an emotive or psychic impulse in search of a political expression. Perhaps the most powerful emotive impulse is vengeance, whether as a result of a perceived injustice or indignity or an act of humiliation.

Such powerful emotive impulses are often individuated, internalized, and personalized by affected individuals leading to acts of self-destruction where the unworthy self becomes the target for retribution of perceived wrongs. The act of externalizing these emotive impulses may be facilitated by political rhetoric that emphasizes the commonality of the aggrieved and a common source of grievances. In this politicization of vengeance and other, lesser forms grievance, the rationalization of externalization and the identification of targets for retribution find expression in a common political perspective and agenda for action.

Common emotional impulses provide the impetus for overcoming collective action problems among politically disempowered individuals. The immediate and direct goal of such emotive action is to establish the capacity to "strike back." Although the impetus to "strike back" implies grievance and, thus, a desire for political change, the immediate and realizable goal is to inflict hurt, not to effect change. The politics of terror, in this instance, are imposed from the outside, recast on the inside, and redirected toward an external target. This emotive, relational quality makes (non-repressive) terrorist action less amenable to rational deterrent strategies. Deterrent actions can be viewed as consistent with, and therefore validation of, the structures of perceived injustice and very often widen the scope of persons directly affected by the actions of authorities and, so, can actually stimulate rather than deter further acts of terrorism.

It can be seen that it is the political quality of common experience, the common attribution of causal agent or target, and the collective coordination, or mobilization, of emotive response that differentiates (non-repressive) organized terrorist action from lesser forms of terror, such as psychotic, sociopathic, or criminal violence. Even these lesser (less-politicized) forms of terror can create a climate of terrorism that has serious effects on social relations, especially when those ostensibly random non-organized acts of disturbed individuals attain a sense of regularity and arbitrariness.

For example, psychotic and sociopathic terror have become more extreme and regularized in US society such that hardly a week goes by without news of another attack on a school or a multiple murder-suicide. This form of terror is much closer to most Americans and is likely to have produced more diffuse effects than the more dramatic but far less frequent form of political terrorism that has culminated in the September , , events and the subsequent "war on terrorism" in Afghanistan. Similarly, terror does not need to be premeditated as is evidenced in the regularity of "spontaneous" Hindu-Muslim riots in India.

Such communal pogroms are not unique to this context but have been, and continue to be, a fairly common method used to maintain power asymmetries in situations of communal competition. Purely sociopathic terrorism, such as the anarchist groups that have operated in Western democracies, are particularly difficult to sustain as they lack sufficient emotive strength (they are steeped mainly in malaise, disaffection, and indignation) and, by nature of their ideological perspective, can not define a common political agenda other than the destruction of the existing order.

Organized terror, while it can be orchestrated to a certain extent among "violence sycophants" (i.e., those individuals who are predisposed to value and commit violence), is most problematic when it achieves a broad network of popular support. Even the "super-empowered individual" who ultimately "pulls the trigger" requires a relatively broad base of support in order to ensure secrecy long enough to realize their full capacity for technological empowerment. Although greater and more accessible technologies of destruction make possible greater power to the individual actor, the preparation of such technologies for actual implementation draw greater aversion, publicity, and attention. Terror requires secrecy and secrecy demands silence not only by those who are integral to the conspiracy but, also, all potential witnesses (i.e., the "sea" in which the "fish" must swim).

Silence is sometimes a function of ignorance (particularly in the first instance of a new form of terrorist action) but is most often achieved through popular, supportive, and cooperative behavior. As such, most terrorist cells operate in close association with larger, more conventional political associations that are sympathetic with the terrorists' political rhetoric and agenda but uncomfortable with the terrorists' methods.

Equally important to the instrumental and operational aspects of broad, popular support is the creation of a supportive rhetorical environment in which extremist rhetoric may reverberate, amplify, and escalate over time. Terrorism, as a political act, stands at once at the nexus between individual and collective action, the emotional and rational, the conventional and the unconventional. It is can be the strongest form of protest or the weakest form of rebellion or a specialized tactic in warfare. Above all else, it is the most personal form of violence.

The nature and quality of the association between the tactical terrorist organization and the larger support network are crucial in defining the scope, efficacy, resilience, and persistence of terrorist activity. Carr makes a particularly strong argument regarding the "galvanizing" effects of terrorist tactics on the strategic interactions between contending groups. Rather than undermining, intimidating, or disabling the will to support contention, the intentional targeting of noncombatant populations, that is the actual, potential, or imagined oppositional support base, further polarizes the contending groups and strengthens and fortifies the affected group's collective resolve to resist and/or strike back.

Carr claims this as compelling evidence of the inevitable failure of terror. Like the myth of the Hydra, terrorist organization tends to recreate and regenerate itself in direct response to the strength of coercive attempts to thwart its activities and remove its leaders or operatives: as one head is removed, several others appear to take its place. Even when the organizational structure is broken completely in a mass sweep of operatives, if there is no attendant change in the underlying conditions that gave rise to the original terrorist psyche, the organization of affected individuals will most likely be recreated over a period of time and such activity will reemerge.

This is surely the general experience of brutal dictatorships and a large part of the reason why these forms of governance are inherently unstable, giving way eventually to more open and less coercive forms of governance. This is also the lesson of the use of "right-wing death squads" in places such as El Salvador, Colombia, and Algeria that create great death, injury, and mayhem but are ineffective in quelling dissent, even when great care is taken to identify and target the leadership cadres of the opposition. It is surely the lesson of the Israeli-Palestinian terrorist conflict which has continued in various forms for seventy years or more.

The strong emotive quality of terrorism is at once a powerful motivating and an inherently limiting factor. Terror is a dynamic, transitional quality that rarely exists for long periods of time without transforming to or integrating with more complex forms of instrumental conflict behavior. The strength of our emotional responses tends to wane over time unless transferred to hate. More often, strong emotional responses stimulate the search for rationality; in this application repeated, or re-stimulated, emotional responses can be very important in sustaining levels of activity.

The greatest threat of terrorism lay not in its capacity to threaten, and deliver, personalized violence but, rather, in its relation to the more institutionalized forms of violence. Terrorist activity is commonly associated, as Carr argues, with all forms of warfare. It is a common instrument in separatist violence, used both by government authorities and separatist agents. Terrorism's greatest strategic value may lay in its demonstration effects, that is, its capacity for signaling both the group's strength and resolve and the target's complicities and vulnerabilities.

Terrorism—Goals and Motivations

Terrorism may not be successful in achieving tangible political goals, but, through its capacity to galvanize public opinion, it may be instrumental in polarizing contending groups and stimulating group members to increase their support for more conventional tactics such as protest or the transformation of protest to open, armed rebellion. These conventional conflict strategies are generally more acceptable alternatives to terrorist activities.

Where terrorism exists without ties to these more collective forms of conflict, it is generally due to one of two reasons: terrorism, as a limited form of engagement, more quickly and effectively overcomes collective action problems that may retard or thwart the mobilization of mass conventional action or state repression may prevent the formation of mass movements, in which case terrorism may be the only available avenue for demonstrations of dissent. Terrorist activity is often the prelude to the transformation of non-violent protest movements to armed rebellion. The transformation of protest to armed conflict provides a tactical niche for acts of terrorism.

The emotive content of terrorist motivation makes it compatible with both political, as argued above, and spiritual rationalizations or justifications. Terrorist activity can be doubly emotive as the moral and ethical dimensions of terrorist action have to be reconciled in the mind of the terrorist.

The sole redeeming quality, so to speak, of the theocratic rationalization is that it is at once empowering and restraining. The appeal to cosmic authorization implies recognition that the contemplated deed is wrong and regretted and that the course of remedial action must be "fit" within the theological parameters of spiritual beliefs in divine benevolence. Purely secular (political) rationalizations of terror may not provide either of these inhibiting qualities: the recognition of transgression and the need for redemption. The recent examples of Nazism and Communism verify this apprehension regarding the qualities of purely human rationalizations of "social engineering".

The contemporary predominance of secular government also contributes to the utility of sectarian rationalizations of dissent as accentuating the moral divide between an unjust temporal authority and aspirations for an idcal and just society in its place. This separation of "state and church" may also help to explain the recent claims of analysts, like Hoffman, that "terrorist incidents perpetrated for religious motives result in so many more deaths [than those with purely political motives]."Such claims are based on statistical artifacts generated by selection biases in data collection.

From this brief discussion of the various conceptualizations of terrorism, a common thread seems to emerge from which the core elements of an operational definition of the terrorist action may be identified. The essential defining quality of terrorism is that it is a direct and intentional violation of the intrinsic vulnerability of the human condition; in the context of the modern state and its structures of collective security this translates into the intentional targeting of civilian, non-combatant populations.

As McKeogh explains, "It is because it is a breach of the principle of non-combatant immunity that terrorism is forthrightly condemned: its wrongness consists primarily in the fact that it targets, not military installations and personnel, but civilian ones." This essential quality has two fundamental political forms which derive from the prevailing structures of authority in societal systems and are part of the same strategic interaction process: repressive (state) and expressive (non-state) terrorism. The underlying assumption of terrorism is that it is a primarily emotive, rather than rational, action in direct pursuit of psychic, rather than, material goals.

Factors that contribute to determining the strength and persistence of the "terror" produced by violence against non-combatant populations include the dramatic, shocking (i.e., extraordinary) impact of the attack(s); the intensity of media coverage; the frequency, lethality, and arbitrariness of the attacks; the perceived potential for future attacks, and the recognized connections between individualized acts of contention and collective action.

The historical record of terrorism seems to indicate that it is becoming less ordinary, that there is a strong negative relationship between the scope and frequency of terrorism and the pace of societal development in specific locations and that the general trend has been a gradual decrease in the scope and frequency of terrorism over the course of evolution of human societies. An important caveat is the positive relationship between the destructive capabilities of terrorism and the general extent and pace of technological development: the "super-empowered terrorist." Think, for example, of the very powerful, subliminal terrorism produced by the growing availability of the technologies of mass destruction and the fear that these weapons may fall into the hands of ill intent.

Types of Terrorism

In early 1975, the Law Enforcement Assistant Administration in the United States formed the National Advisory Committee on Criminal Justice Standards and Goals. One of the five volumes that the committee wrote was entitled *Disorders and Terrorism*, produced by the Task Force on Disorders and Terrorism under the direction of H.H.A. Cooper, Director of the Task Force staff. The Task Force classified terrorism into six categories.

— *Civil disorder*—A form of collective violence interfering with the peace, security, and normal functioning of the community.

— *Political terrorism*—Violent criminal behaviour designed primarily to generate fear in the community, or substantial segment of it, for political purposes.

— *Non-Political terrorism*—Terrorism that is not aimed at political purposes but which exhibits "conscious design to create and maintain a high degree of fear for coercive purposes, but the end is individual or collective gain rather than the achievement of a political objective."

— *Quasi-terrorism*—The activities incidental to the commission of crimes of violence that are similar in form and method to genuine terrorism but which nevertheless lack its essential ingredient. It is not the main purpose of the quasi-terrorists to induce terror in the immediate victim as in the case of genuine terrorism, but the quasi-terrorist uses the modalities and techniques of the genuine terrorist and produces similar consequences and reaction. For example, the fleeing felon who takes hostages is a quasi-terrorist, whose methods are similar to those of the genuine terrorist but whose purposes are quite different.

- *Limited political terrorism*—Genuine political terrorism is characterized by a revolutionary approach; limited political terrorism refers to "acts of terrorism which are committed for ideological or political motives but which are not part of a concerted campaign to capture control of the state.
- *Official or state terrorism*–"referring to nations whose rule is based upon fear and oppression that reach similar to terrorism or such proportions." It may also be referred to as Structural Terrorism defined broadly as terrorist acts carried out by governments in pursuit of political objectives, often as part of their foreign policy.

Several sources have further defined the typology of terrorism:

- Political terrorism
- Sub-state terrorism
- Social revolutionary terrorism
- Nationalist-separatist terrorism
- Religious extremist terrorism
- Religious fundamentalist Terrorism
- New religions terrorism
- Right-wing terrorism
- Left-wing terrorism

— Single-issue terrorism
— State-sponsored terrorism
— Regime or state terrorism
— Criminal terrorism
— Pathological terrorism

Domestic Terrorism

The relationship between domestic terrorism and democracy is very complex. Terrorism is most common in nations with intermediate political freedom, and is least common in the most democratic nations. However, one study suggests that suicide terrorism may be an exception to this general rule. Evidence regarding this particular method of terrorism reveals that every modern suicide campaign has targeted a democracy--a state with a considerable degree of political freedom. The study suggests that concessions awarded to terrorists during the 1980s and 1990s for suicide attacks increased their frequency.

Some examples of "terrorism" in non-democracies include ETA in Spain under Francisco Franco, the Shining Path in Peru under Alberto Fujimori, the Kurdistan Workers Party when Turkey was ruled by military leaders and the ANC in South Africa. Democracies, such as the United Kingdom, United States, Israel, Indonesia, India, Spain and the Philippines, have also experienced domestic terrorism.

While a democratic nation espousing civil liberties may claim a sense of higher moral ground than other regimes, an act of terrorism within such a state may cause a dilemma: whether to maintain its civil liberties and thus risk being perceived as ineffective in dealing with the problem; or alternatively to restrict its civil liberties and thus risk delegitimizing its claim of supporting civil liberties. This dilemma, some social theorists would conclude, may very well play into the initial plans of the acting terrorist(s); namely, to delegitimize the state.

Religious Terrorism

Religious terrorism is terrorism performed by groups or individuals, the motivation of which is typically rooted in the faith based tenets. Terrorist acts throughout the centuries have been performed on religious grounds with the hope to either spread or enforce a system of belief, viewpoint or opinion. Religious terrorism does not in itself necessarily define a specific religious standpoint or view, but instead usually defines an individual or a group view or interpretation of that belief system's teachings.

PERPETRATORS OF TERRORISM

The perpetrators of acts of terrorism can be individuals, groups, or states. According to some definitions, clandestine or semi-clandestine state actors may also carry out terrorist acts outside the framework of a state of war. However, the most common image of terrorism is that it is carried out by small and secretive cells, highly motivated to serve a particular cause and many of the most deadly operations in recent times, such as the September 11 attacks, the London underground bombing, and the 2002 Bali bombing were planned and carried out by a close clique, composed of close friends, family members and other strong social networks. These groups benefited from the free flow of information and efficient telecommunications to succeed where others had failed.

Over the years, many people have attempted to come up with a terrorist profile to attempt to explain these individuals' actions through their psychology and social circumstances. Others, like Roderick Hindery, have sought to discern profiles in the propaganda tactics used by terrorists. Some security organizations designate these groups as *violent non-state actors*. A 2007 study by economist Alan B. Krueger found that terrorists were less likely to come from an impoverished background (28% vs. 33%) and more likely to have at least a high-school education (47% vs. 38%). Another analysis found only 16% of terrorists came from impoverished families, vs. 30% of male Palestinians, and over 60% had gone beyond high school, vs. 15% of the populace.

To avoid detection, a terrorist will look, dress, and behave normally until executing the assigned mission. Some claim that attempts to profile terrorists based on personality, physical, or sociological traits are not useful. The physical and behavioral description of the terrorist could describe almost any normal person. However, the majority of terrorist attacks are carried out by military age men, aged 16–40.

State Sponsors

A state can sponsor terrorism by funding or harboring a terrorist organization. Opinions as to which acts of violence by states consist of state-sponsored terrorism vary widely. When states provide funding for groups considered by some to be terrorist, they rarely acknowledge them as such.

State Terrorism

As with "terrorism" the concept of "state terrorism" is controversial. The Chairman of the United Nations Counter-Terrorism Committee has stated that the Committee was conscious of 12 international Conventions on the subject, and none of them referred to State terrorism, which was not an international legal concept. If States abused their power, they should be judged against international conventions dealing with war crimes, international human rights and international humanitarian law. Former United Nations Secretary-General Kofi Annan has said that it is "time to set aside debates on so-called 'state terrorism'. The use of force by states is already thoroughly regulated under international law" However, he also made clear that, "regardless of the differences between governments on the question of definition of terrorism, what is clear and what we can all agree on is any deliberate attack on innocent civilians, regardless of one's cause, is unacceptable and fits into the definition of terrorism."

State terrorism has been used to refer to terrorist acts by governmental agents or forces. This involves the use of state resources employed by a state's foreign policies, such as using its military to directly perform acts of terrorism. Professor of Political Science Michael Stohl cites the examples that include Germany's bombing of London and the U.S. atomic destruction of Hiroshima during World War II. He argues that "the use of terror tactics is common in international relations and the state has been and remains a more likely employer of terrorism within the international system than insurgents." They also cite the First strike option as an example of the "terror of coercive diplomacy" as a form of this, which holds the world hostage with the implied threat of using nuclear weapons in "crisis management." They argue that the institutionalized form of terrorism has occurred as a result of changes that took place following World War II. In this analysis, state terrorism exhibited as a form of foreign policy was shaped by the presence and use of weapons of mass destruction, and that the legitimizing of such violent behavior led to an increasingly accepted form of this state behavior.

State terrorism has also been used to describe peacetime actions by governmental agents such as the bombing of Pan Am Flight 103. Charles Stewart Parnell described William Ewart Gladstone's Irish Coercion Act as terrorism in his "no-Rent manifesto" in 1881, during the Irish Land War. The concept is also used to describe political repressions by governments against their own civilian population with the purpose to incite fear. For example, taking and executing civilian hostages or extrajudicial elimination campaigns are commonly considered "terror" or terrorism, for example during the Red Terror or Great Terror. Such actions are often also described as democide or genocide which has been argued to be equivalent to state terrorism. Empirical studies on this have found that democracies have little democide.

Funding

State sponsors have constituted a major form of funding; for example, PLO, DFLP and some other terrorist groups were funded by the Soviet Union.

"Revolutionary tax" is another major form of funding, and essentially a euphemism for "protection money". Revolutionary taxes are typically extorted from businesses, and they also "play a secondary role as one other means of intimidating the target population".

Other major sources of funding include kidnapping for ransoms, smuggling, fraud and robbery.

Tactics of Terrorism

While terrorists act according to different motivations and goals, all such groups have one tactic in common: intimidation or coercion of the public or the government in order to effect social or political change. Terrorism uses violence, or threat of violence, against one portion of a society to compel the greater body of that society or their leaders to make a change out of fear. Terrorism often exploits propaganda techniques to ensure the public receives the intended message. The term Propaganda of the Deed, coined by Malatesta, Cafiero, and Covelli, states that the message is most strongly conveyed through violence.

In the media, terrorist violence is most commonly portrayed as being carried out via an improvised explosive device, although chemical weapons have been used on occasion. Vehicles from pick-up trucks to planes, like in the September 11, 2001 attacks, have been used as guided incendiary device. In the failed 2002 airliner attack shoulder-launched surface-to-air missiles were fired at an airliner while taking off. Concerns have also been raised regarding attacks involving nuclear weapons or biological weapons.

However, despite the popular image of terrorism as bombings alone, and the large number of casualties and higher media impact associated with bombings, conventional firearms are as much if not more pervasive in their use. In 2004, the European Council recognized the "need to ensure terrorist organisations and groups are starved of the components of their trade," including "the need to ensure greater security of firearms, explosives, bomb-making equipment and technologies that contribute to the perpetration of terrorist outrages."

Terrorist groups may arrange for secondary devices to detonate at a slightly later time in order to kill emergency-response personnel attempting to attend to the dead and wounded. Repeated or suspected use of secondary devices can also delay emergency response out of concern that such devices may exist. Examples include a (failed) device that was meant to release cyanide-gas during the February 26, 1993 World Trade Center bombing; and a second car bomb that detonated 20 minutes after the December 1, 2001 Ben Yehuda Street Bombing by Hamas in Jerusalem.

Training

There are and have been training camps for terrorists, The range of training depends greatly on the level of support the terrorist organization receives from various organizations and states. In nearly every case the training incorporates the philosophy and agenda of the groups leadership as justification for the training as well as the potential acts of terrorism which may be committed. State sanctioned training is by far the most extensive and thorough, often employing professional soldiers and covert operatives of the supporting state.

Preparation

Preparation of a major attack such as the September 11, 2001 attacks may take years, whereas a simpler attack, depending on the availability of arms,resources,and more it may be almost spontaneous.

Cover

Where terrorism occurs in the context of open warfare or insurgency, its perpetrators may shelter behind a section of the local population. Examples include the intifada on Israeli-occupied territory, and insurgency in Iraq. This population, which may be ethnically distinct from the counter-terrorist forces, is either sympathetic to their cause, indifferent, or acts under duress.

Terrorists preparing for the September 11, 2001 attacks changed their appearance to avoid looking radical.

Funding

Funding can be raised in both legal and illegal ways. Some of the most common ways to raise funds are through front groups, charitable organizations, or NGOs with similar ideologies. In the absence of state funding, terrorists may rely on organized crime to fund their activities. This has included kidnapping, drug trafficking, or robbery. Additionally, terrorists have also found many more sources of revenue.

Communication

Even though old-school communication methods like radio are still used, the revolution in communication technology over the past 10-15 years has dramatically changed how terrorist organizations communicate. E-mails, fax transmissions, websites, cell phones, and satellite telephones have made it possible for organizations to contemplate a global strategy. However, too great a reliance on this new technology leaves organizations vulnerable to sophisticated monitoring of communication and triangulation of its source.

Terrorism and Human Rights

The issue of terrorism and human rights has long been a concern of the United Nations human rights program, but it has become more urgent following the attack of 11 September 2001 on the United States of America and the worldwide surge in acts of terrorism. OHCHR condemns terrorism unequivocally and recognises the duty of States to protect those living within their jurisdictions from terrorism. The Office of the High Commissioner for Human Rights has placed a priority on protection of human rights, notably the right to life, and the question of protecting human rights in the context of counter-terrorism measures.

The Secretary-General, the High Commissioner for Human Rights, and others in the UN system have emphasised that human rights norms must be rigorously respected by all, including in states of emergency. As Secretary-General Kofi Annan stated at a special meeting of the Security Council's Counter-Terrorism Committee with International, Regional, and Sub-Regional Organisations, on 6 March 2003, "Our responses to terrorism, as well as our efforts to thwart it and prevent it, should uphold the human rights that terrorists aim to destroy. Respect for human rights, fundamental freedoms and the rule of law are essential tools in the effort to combat terrorism—not privileges to be sacrificed at a time of tension."

On 28 September 2001, the Security Council adopted Resolution 1373 under Chapter VII of the UN Charter, obligating States to implement more effective counter-terrorism measures at the national level and to increase international cooperation in the struggle against terrorism. The resolution created the Counter-Terrorism Committee (CTC) to monitor action on this issue and to receive reports from States on measures taken.

Former High Commissioner Mary Robinson and the late High Commissioner Sergio Vieira de Mello both addressed the CTC, urging it to take account of human rights in its review of counter-terrorism measures. Mr. Vieira de Mello, speaking to the CTC in October 2002, stated his conviction that "the best - the only - strategy to isolate and defeat terrorism is by respecting human rights, fostering social justice, enhancing democracy and upholding the primacy of the rule of law." Since then, the CTC and the UN Human Rights Committee have exchanged briefings on their working methods and areas of concern.

In resolution 1456, the Security Council declared that "States must ensure that any measure taken to combat terrorism comply with all their obligations under international law, and should adopt such measures in accordance with international law, in particular international human rights, refugee, and humanitarian law." Human rights law has sought to strike a fair balance between legitimate national security concerns and the protection of fundamental freedoms. It acknowledges that States must address serious and genuine security concerns, such as terrorism. The balance is reflected in the International Covenant on Civil and Political Rights (ICCPR) as well as in regional instruments.

Threats to national security may, under very specific conditions, lead to a state of emergency under which certain rights are subject to derogation (suspension). However, certain rights are never subject to derogation. The question of states of emergency and derogation is addressed in article 4 of the ICCPR. In July 2001, the UN Human Rights Committee adopted General Comment No. 29, concerning ICCPR article 4, in which it clarified the scope of non-derogable rights and identified elements which cannot be subject to lawful derogation. Despite the importance of the fight against terrorism, some UN human rights bodies have expressed concern that counter-terrorism measures may infringe on human rights. For example, UN special rapporteurs and independent experts, at their annual meeting in Geneva in June 2003, adopted the following joint statement .

The special rapporteurs and independent experts express alarm at the growing threats against human rights, threats that necessitate a renewed resolve to defend and promote these rights. They also note the impact of this environment on the effectiveness and independence of special procedures.

Although they share in the unequivocal condemnation of terrorism, they voice profound concern at the multiplication of policies, legislation and practices increasingly being adopted by many countries in the name of the fight against terrorism which affect negatively the enjoyment of virtually all human rights - civil, cultural, economic, political and social.

They draw attention to the dangers inherent in the indiscriminate use of the term "terrorism", and the resulting new categories of discrimination. They recall that, in accordance with the International Covenant on Civil and Political Rights and pursuant to the Convention against Torture and Other Cruel, Inhuman or Degrading Treatment or Punishment, certain rights are non-derogable and that any measures of derogation from the other rights guaranteed by the Covenant must be made in strict conformity with the provisions of its article 4.

The special rapporteurs and independent experts deplore the fact that, under the pretext of combating terrorism, human rights defenders are threatened and vulnerable groups are targeted and discriminated against on the basis of origin and socio-economic status, in particular migrants, refugees and asylum-seekers, indigenous peoples and people fighting for their land rights or against the negative effects of economic globalisation policies.

They strongly affirm that any measures taken by States to combat terrorism must be in accordance with States' obligations under the international human rights instruments. They are determined, in the framework of their respective mandates, to monitor and investigate developments in this area and call upon all those committed to respect for human rights, including the United Nations, to be vigilant to prevent any abuse of counter-terrorism measures.

OHCHR action on the issue of human rights and terrorism is guided in part by General Assembly resolution 58/187 (2003) and Commission on Human Rights resolution 2003/68 ("Protection of human rights and fundamental freedoms while countering terrorism"). These resolutions call on the High Commissioner's office to:

a) examine the question of the protection of human rights and fundamental freedoms while countering terrorism, taking into account reliable information from all sources;

b) make general recommendations concerning the obligation of States to promote and protect human rights and fundamental freedoms while taking actions to counter terrorism; and

c) provide assistance and advice to States, upon their request, on the protection of human rights and fundamental freedoms while countering terrorism, as well as to relevant United Nations bodies.

The issue of human rights and terrorism is also addressed in General Assembly resolution 58/174 (2003) and Commission on Human Rights resolution 2003/37 ("Human rights and terrorism").

The Office also implements the findings of the Secretary-General's Policy Working Group on Terrorism, in particular its sub-group on human rights and terrorism. Based on a Policy Working Group recommendation, the Office published in 2003 the Digest of Jurisprudence of the UN and Regional Organisations on the Protection of Human Rights while Countering Terrorism. The Digest, which is available as an OHCHR publication, makes several important contributions, for example by clarifying the concept of non-derogable rights under both the United Nations and regional human rights systems.

It addresses the core principles of necessity and proportionality, which are fundamental to lawful counter-terrorism measures. Through excerpts from findings of the UN and regional human rights bodies, the Digest shows concerns that have been expressed over practices which are in use or under consideration by States today, such as the use of military tribunals to try civilians, and detention practices which disregard recognised international standards.

In 1997, the Sub-Commission on the Promotion and Protection of Human Rights recommended the appointment of a Special Rapporteur to conduct a comprehensive study on human rights and terrorism. The Special Rapporteur has submitted a series of reports to the Sub-Commission since then. International attention became focused on terrorism with the attack on World Trade Centre twin towers and

Pentagon on September11, 2001. Since it was the first time that such attacks were experienced by the USA on its surface, it shook up the entire country from the President downwards. And for the first time terrorism became a four letter word in the USA. The citizen on the street and the entire power structure of the USA felt humiliated at the gall of the attackers.

A similar incident, back home, was the attack on Indian Parliament on December 13, 2001.Here the situation was different in the sense that for the first time such a serious attack was mounted on the symbol of Indian Republic in the capital of the country. It gave the government a powerful argument in favour of 'streamlining' and 'providing more teeth' to the existing anti-terror laws. The power structure of our country did not react qualitatively very different from the power structure of the United States except that the latter was in a position to take independent decisions in its interest unhindered by any other limitations. The power structure of our country felt strengthened in its pleadings in the court of the USA against Pakistan.

The international bulwark of joint action concerning any development that impinges on the international law rightfully belongs to the United Nations. The new situation created by the attack on the twin towers exposed the impotence of the world body and underlined the position of the USA as an undeclared rival of the United Nations. On the home turf, the government received widespread popular support in favour of the existing laws designated as 'anti terror laws' and a fillip to adopt more such measures with the result that in the general atmosphere created by this attack in favour of license to curtail liberties, the attempts to browbeat and suppress the media, Indian and foreign, did not evoke much protest.

Even when those elected representatives who had supported such 'anti-terrorism' laws in the Parliament were themselves detained under these laws there was not much hue and cry against it. While in the USA the brunt of anti-terrorism steps was borne by the foreigners, mainly the foreigners from Asian countries, in India it fell on the common citizen. It had happened in the past also when the TADA was in operation. It was widely applied on trade union workers, political activists, and defenders of Human Rights.

One fallout of the United States campaign against terrorism was destruction of Afghanistan and conversion of Pakistan into one of the bases for mounting attacks on Afghanistan, compelling the country to completely reverse its policy vis-à-vis Taliban Afghanistan. There are strong possibilities at present (which may turn into a reality by the time these lines appear in print) that the USA may start a second war against Iraq. How far is the USA concerned with containing Iraq in its 'criminal' intentions and how far is it concerned with its oil is an important question. It is also important to note that it has been made clear that while the USA has the right to pre-emptive strikes, India (or for that matter Pakistan) does not.

The point to be noted here is that while all anti-terrorism fortifications, technological and armament based, in countries in the Asian sub-continent and the limited wars as anti-terrorism steps, prove a tremendous strain on the economy of such countries, they result in a huge surplus creation for the American armament industry. Such situations, therefore, receive solid backing of the American politico-economic structure. As other under developed countries step up the process of equipping for 'containing and facing terrorist acts' the American economy, and also the economics of its European allies, net increased demand in these fields. Limited wars between two under developed countries or against such a country by the U.S. creates increased demands in Defence Industries of the U.S. and its allies.

The Armament industry thrives during such wars. Armaments are produced for destruction and are needed again and again as the war goes on. The relationship of the development of capitalist countries and the resources and markets of the underdeveloped countries has been forcefully laid bare by political and economic thinkers like A.A. Berle, John Kenneth Galbraith, Paul A Baran, Paul A Sweezy, and others. The above may appear a disjointed narration but there is a binding string running right through. In today's unipolar world scene anti-terrorism campaigns, especially those emanating from the U.S.A., cannot be separated from globalisation and the end aim turns out to be service of American economy.

Some laws restrict even human rights as defined by the United Nations. True, some restrictions may be inevitable because society in the real world is not Utopia as visualised by Sir Thomas More wherein everything is perfect or idealistic and all the citizens are selfless. The spirit of capitalism, today's reigning philosophy, derives from selfishness of human beings. In a society of self-less citizens Capitalism will fail. Capitalism has to have laws to safeguard the selfish spirit of the individual. It is not called individualism for nothing.

One person's rights ends where the other person's rights begin. We have to be clear and conscious, therefore, that when we make a law and restrict the freedoms of the citizens, the restrictions have to be minimum, well defined, and open to justiciability. There have to be clear and strong safe guards and the restrictions have to be, the especially in the case of human rights, temporary.

In today's scenario we have also to see whether our laws serve our interests. The interests of an under developed country may clash with the interest of developed countries, though their will always be grey areas. Such a situation needs fearless and honest leadership. We have to beware that compelled by globalisation or 'need to curb terrorism' we may not be surviving the interest of the developed world. Just as terrorism is temporary, curbs on human rights also have to be temporary as human rights are permanent.

In short, the argument, we have to understand that every act of terrorism infringes on the human rights of the people. We also have to accept that laws restrict rights of the people, necessarily or unnecessarily. But we have to be clear that we have to define terrorism in the context of our country and have to devise temporary limitations on the rights of the people.

COUNTER-TERRORISM

Counter-terrorism is the practices, tactics, techniques, and strategies that governments, militaries, police departments and corporations adopt to prevent or in response to terrorist threats and/or acts, both real and imputed.

The tactic of terrorism is available to insurgents and governments. Not all insurgents use terror as a tactic, and some choose not to use it because other tactics work better for them in a particular context. Individuals, such as Timothy McVeigh, may also engage in terrorist acts such as the Oklahoma City bombing.

If the terrorism is part of a broader insurgency, counter-terrorism may also form a part of a counter-insurgency doctrine, but political, economic, and other measures may focus more on the insurgency than the specific acts of terror. Foreign internal defense (FID) is a term used by several countries for programs either to suppress insurgency, or reduce the conditions under which insurgency could develop.

Counter-terrorism includes both the detection of potential acts and the response to related events.

The concept of anti-terrorism emerges from a thorough examining of the concept of terrorism as well as an attempt to understand and articulate what constitutes terrorism in Western terms. In military contexts, terrorism is a tactic, not an ideology. Terrorism may be a tactic in a war between nation-states, in a civil war, or in an insurgency.

Counter-terrorism refers to offensive strategies intended to prevent a belligerent, in a broader conflict, from successfully using the tactic of terrorism. The US military definition, compatible with the definitions used by NATO and many other militaries, is "Operations that include the offensive measures taken to prevent, deter, preempt, and respond to terrorism." In other words, counter-terrorism is a set of techniques for denying an opponent the use of terrorism-based tactics, just as counter-air is a set of techniques for denying the opponent the use of attack aircraft.

Anti-terrorism is defensive, intended to reduce the chance of an attack using terrorist tactics at specific points, or to reduce the vulnerability of possible targets to such tactics. "*Defensive measures used to reduce the vulnerability of individuals and property to terrorist acts, to include limited response and containment by local military and civilian forces.*"

To continue the analogy between air and terrorist capability, offensive counter-air missions attack the airfields of the opponent, while defensive counter-air uses antiaircraft missiles to protect a point on one's own territory. The ongoing Israeli-Palestinian conflict, Sri Lankan Civil War, and Colombian Civil War are examples of conflicts where terrorism is present, along with other tactics, so that participants use counter- and anti-terrorism to limit the opponent's use of terror tactics

Building a counter-terrorism plan involves all segments of a society or many government agencies. In dealing with foreign terrorists, the lead responsibility is usually at the national level. Because propaganda and indoctrination lie at the core of terrorism, understanding their profile and functions increases the ability to counter terrorism more effectively.

Most counter-terrorism strategies involve an increase in standard police and domestic intelligence. The central activities are traditional: interception of communications, and the tracing of persons. New technology has, however, expanded the range of military and law enforcement operations.

Domestic intelligence is often directed at specific groups, defined on the basis of origin or religion, which is a source of political controversy. Mass surveillance of an entire population raises objections on civil liberties grounds.

To select the effective action when terrorism appears to be more of an isolated event, the appropriate government organizations need to understand the source, motivation, methods of preparation, and tactics of terrorist groups. Good intelligence is at the heart of such preparation, as well as political and social understanding of any grievances that might be solved. Ideally, one gets information from inside the group, a very difficult challenge for HUMINT because operational terrorist cells are often small, with all members known to one another, perhaps even related.

Counterintelligence is a great challenge with the security of cell-based systems, since the ideal, but nearly impossible, goal is to obtain a clandestine source within the cell. Financial tracking can play a role, as can communications intercept, but both of these approaches need to be balanced against legitimate expectations of privacy.